Rehearsal
Management
for Directors

Rehearsal Management for Directors

David Alberts

HEINEMANN
Portsmouth, NH

Heinemann
A division of Reed Elsevier Inc.
361 Hanover Street
Portsmouth, NH 03801-3912

Offices and agents throughout the world

Library of Congress Cataloging-in-Publication Data
Alberts, David.
    Rehearsal management for directors / David Alberts.
       p. cm.
    Includes bibliographical references.
    ISBN 0-435-08665-0
    1. Theater rehearsals. 2. Theater—Production and direction. I. Title.
PN2071.R45A43 1995
792.0233—dc20   94-49122
                                                            CIP

Editor: Lisa A. Barnett
Production: Vicki Kasabian
Cover design: Mary Cronin

Printed in the United States of America on acid-free paper
04 03   DA   3   4   5

Contents

Preface

The director's mission can be simply stated: to bring theatre to life, and to bring life to the theatre. The task is not simple, however, nor is it simply done, as anyone who has ever directed a play or musical will readily attest.

Producing a play begins with a thought, an idea, a vision. In time, that vision begins to take on a recognizable, artistic form in the hands of the director, designers, cast, and crew. The director's role in the production process is that of practical visionary. Through his or her own considerable efforts and by effectively channeling the efforts of others in all areas of the production, the director brings the collective vision of the production to life in front of an audience, as the true culmination of the artistic experience.

This book began as an answer to a question: *How do you make a rehearsal schedule?* The question came from a theatre student—a dedicated graduate student—who had taken the usual regimen of undergraduate and graduate courses in acting and directing and had directed several acting scenes and a few one-act plays along the way. Faced with directing a full-length play for the first time in her life, she had little idea of where or how to begin the process and little comprehension of the scope of the undertaking.

That simple and straightforward question—*How do you make a rehearsal schedule?*—required a not-so-simple response. We sat down together and discussed the entire production process, beginning to end, from preproduction planning to postproduction evaluation. Much of this was a revelation to her, particularly the managerial and business-oriented aspects. We discussed organizational management, staffing, budgeting, auditioning, casting, developing rehearsal time lines, integrating design and technical elements into the production—and I learned that many of these topics had never been discussed, or had been discussed only briefly, in her theatre classes.

I am indebted to that graduate student (thank you, Joanne) for providing the principal motivation for this book. Her question and others like it have been asked of me and of other directors many, many times. While it is true that certain artistic elements of directing can be learned only through experience, many practical elements of directing a play or musical can be learned beforehand and then applied directly to the production process. This book provides that practical information.

A number of people are due special thanks for their invaluable contributions, for their inspiration, and for their support. Among them are Dr. Allen Kepke and Dr. Allen White of the faculty of Bowling Green State University; J. Milton Roberts; Dr. Nancy Wynn Zucchero; my daughter, Morgan; and the many directors, actors, actresses, designers, and technicians, theatre artists all, with whom I've had the privilege of working through the years.

Introduction

*A*s everyone who has been associated with putting on a play or musical knows, a theatrical production is not an intrinsically organized and orderly undertaking, even at its best. Diverse artistic elements and sometimes volatile personalities must somehow be brought together to form a cohesive, unified, artistic production. Some sense of order must be imposed on the chaos and seeming anarchy, and that awesome and sometimes overwhelming responsibility falls to the director.

The role of the modern theatre director has evolved significantly during the latter part of the twentieth century, into one that is complex and highly demanding. Mastery of the director's art and craft no longer ensures success. Today, very few theatre directors "just direct," particularly in the amateur theatre. Directing—the *artistry* of directing—is only one aspect of the modern director's repertoire of necessary skills. More than anything else, directing today is about *leadership*—artistic leadership, certainly, but managerial, motivational, and instructional leadership as well.

The modern director's overriding concern is to mold all the elements of a production into a unified artistic experience. To that end she must undertake a wide range of responsibilities that encompass not only purely artistic matters, but also matters having to do with human resources, budget control, and community relations. The modern titles of director of theatre, managing artistic director, and producing director, among others, attest to the administrative and managerial responsibilities as well as artistic concerns a modern director faces. In a small educational or community theatre, for example, the overall accountability for a production quite often falls to the director. She may be responsible for everything from choosing the play, hiring the staff, designing the set, and selecting the cast to organizing and training the ushers, selling tickets, and occasionally sweeping the stage!

For the most part, directing courses in the theatre training programs of our colleges and universities prepare aspiring directors for the artistic endeavors they will pursue. Very often, however, these training programs provide very little grounding in the more practical aspects of modern theatre making that working directors face every day. Likewise, few directing texts offer anything more than a brief overview of the director's responsibilities outside the artistic and creative realms. The range and depth of responsibilities the theatre director faces today can be quite a revelation to the first-time director who does not have the skills, training, or experience necessary to fulfill all the requirements of the position effectively. Too often, a director's artistic capability is seriously compromised because she is unaware of or doesn't understand the many small but very important "standard operating procedures" of an active theatre organization.

Rehearsal Management for Directors was written as a resource for aspiring directors and more experienced directors alike. It is a guide to the nuts and bolts of directing, the very necessary aspects of the day-to-day realities of directing a play or a musical.

A basic knowledge and understanding of the art and craft of directing is assumed as a prerequisite for using this book effectively. Familiarity with a wide historical range of plays, play production techniques, types of staging, varieties of stage movement, design elements, technical theatre, and styles and methods of actor training is something every director should have at her command. This book will provide the additional practical information that a director needs to be able to direct and manage her production more effectively and more efficiently.

The Director as Manager 1

You are the director. You've assumed the responsibility of directing a theatrical production, the success or failure of which now rests with you. The extremely diverse and occasionally divergent group of talents, abilities, and personalities that you will soon assemble as the designers, cast, and crew of your production will rely on you to help them pull together to produce a show. It is your responsibility, ultimately, to help every one of these people realize her or his full creative potential through what each (and you) hopes will be a unique, remarkable, memorable, and rewarding experience. You have quite possibly been entrusted with the fate of the producing organization as well.

In the best of all possible worlds, you would be responsible solely for the artistic success of the production. As ironic as it may seem, however, how you respond to the challenges of your responsibility on the most basic management level will determine to a very great extent the artistic success or failure of your production. The most successful directors are those who are the best *facilitators*—those who possess both the artistic *and* managerial skills necessary to generate a truly first-rate production. It's not simply a matter of getting your people together, "letting it happen," and hoping for the best. First-rate theatrical productions don't just happen. It's a matter of consciously and purposefully pursuing a singular artistic vision, and of "directing" everyone's efforts toward the realization of that vision.

Directing a play has been likened, at its most basic, to directing traffic. Both a policeman and a director regulate the flow of traffic from one point to another. Both a policeman and a director are out there in the middle of the road, waving their arms, trying to impose some sense of order on what would otherwise devolve into anarchy. Both a policeman and a director must know *how, why,* and *when* to wave their arms, and how to use their arm-waving skills creatively for best effect. Both a policeman and a director bring their experience and their organizational skills to the task at hand. Most important, both a policeman and a director must have a fairly good idea of what the likely result of their arm waving will be.

The difference between directing a play and directing traffic is that as a theatre director your job is to influence all the drivers to go in the same direction, toward *your* destination—your vision for the production—rather than letting them go their separate ways to their own destinations. A director maintains traffic on a one-way street. Your job is to bring everyone in from the side streets and get them all going in the same direction. There is no consistently right way to accomplish this. There are, however, certain skills and abilities that any director must possess to facilitate the flow of traffic successfully.

Above all, directing is about *leadership*—creative leadership *and* organizational leadership. Effective leadership in the theatre—as in any other undertaking, from IBM to the corner grocery store—entails harnessing the maximum amount of imagination through the minimum use of control within clearly defined limits.

In a theatrical production there are two types of limitations: creative and organizational. The creative limitations are essentially the limitations imposed by the script—the basics of plot, character, and theme. The organizational limitations are those imposed on the realization of that script—the budget, production facilities, and staff, for instance.

The director is free to use his expressive and imaginative capabilities to the utmost within those imposed creative and organizational limitations. Too often, however, even experienced directors become so preoccupied with the limitations that they fail to realize the incredible range of opportunities each production offers.

Some directors believe the artistic and organizational limitations imposed on a production severely inhibit their creativity. The truth is quite the opposite. Limitations *enhance* creativity, because they force creative solutions. Effective and imaginative directors consider it a personal and artistic challenge to transcend whatever limitations are imposed. A producer can limit your budget, but he can't limit your imagination.

In any theatrical endeavor the director makes artistic choices—set design, blocking, casting—as well as organizational choices—rehearsal schedule, budget. Every choice, every decision the director makes leads to a particular course of action, which will lead, in turn, to another decision and another course of action. So it goes, throughout the production process. Sometimes the choices you face will appear to be in direct conflict with one another. Your responsibility is to resolve those conflicts as best you can and reconcile the various options within the limitations imposed on you by the script and the producing organization.

The objectives of theatrical producing organizations are not all the same. As a director, it is vital that you know and understand the priorities and the artistic, financial, and in some cases, educational objectives of the producing organization with which you are associated. You cannot hope to fulfill the objectives of your organization and meet the organization's expectations for the production if you have no idea what those objectives and expectations are.

In educational theatre, for example, the emphasis is on training and developing student talent. Since educational theatres are subsidized to a greater or lesser extent by the educational institutions they are part of, there is less emphasis on audience satisfaction—and subsequently less emphasis on the business-oriented aspects of a production—than in any other type of theatrical organization. However, in this era of budget cuts (particularly in the arts) and intensified scrutiny of the fiscal responsibility of our colleges and universities, an increasing number of educational theatre programs have been compelled to become self-supporting, regardless of instructional objectives. Educational administrators, as the "producers," expect at least a minimal return on their "investment," if only enough to break even. They also expect a certain level of audience satisfaction.

Theatre department administrators can no longer minimize the importance of the audience, nor can they rely on a captive audience for support, even on relatively isolated college campuses. Audiences are highly mobile and remarkably discriminating. They want the best return they can get from their cultural dollar, in terms of both artistic merit and entertainment value. If they can't find it on their own campus, they will go elsewhere in search of it.

In community theatre, the emphasis is primarily on audience appeal, but there is at least some attention to business matters. As its designation implies, community theatre exists for the community it serves. Financial stability and a production-to-production, year-to-year continuity are the overriding considerations facing many community theatres. The community theatre must appeal to its audience through its productions in order to engender financial support that will, in turn, ensure its continued existence. If the community as a whole supports the theatre at the box office, and through other forms of financial support, all is well. If the community rejects the offerings of the theatre, or finds them less than satisfactory in terms of audience appeal or artistic merit, the community's interests and expectations must be accommodated if the theatre is to survive.

A professional production company is the most business oriented of all theatrical endeavors. In the professional theatre the emphasis is on financial success. Producers want their productions to be critically acclaimed, of course, as long as the effect of that critical recognition is clearly demonstrated at the box office. The professional theatre is, after all, primarily a business. Most producers consider critical acclaim without financial success to be synonymous with failure.

Some directors feel it is the organization's responsibility to meet the *director's* expectations, rather than the director's responsibility to meet the *organization's* expectations. In an ideal world perhaps this should be so, with the artistic success of a production taking precedence over financial considerations. Unfortunately, this is not an ideal world, and until the prevailing conditions change, a director cannot realistically expect that the organization will fulfill his own hopes and aspirations without first fulfilling its own.

Whatever the type of producing organization—from all-volunteer, amateur community theatre to educational theatre to regional theatre to Broadway—it is important to remember one stark reality: theatre is a business. It is an *artistic* business, yes, but a business nonetheless. Many actors, directors, and designers find this talk about theatre as a business extremely distasteful. Some find it somehow beneath their dignity, as artists, to discuss it. Theatre as a business is also disconcerting to "theatre people" because many of them have little or no real-life business experience.

It is not necessary to hold an MBA from Stanford or Harvard to function as a director in the theatre; it *is* necessary to be aware of, understand, and accept the situation as it exists. If you wish to live and prosper in the theatre, particularly as a director, then you must learn to work *within* the system. This is not to demean your skills and sensibilities nor to deny your artistic standards. It is to encourage you to learn to channel your skills and principles in a constructive and potentially fulfilling way. If you want to play the game, you need to know the rules, and you also need to know how to use the rules to the advantage of your production.

The "Rules"

You already know the first rule . . . like it or not, for better or worse, theatre is a business.

The second important rule that any director must recognize is that theatre is essentially a buyer's market—and that means both for those who provide directorial work in this highly competitive marketplace and for their (and your) potential customers, the audience. For most theatre people, the choice between working and not working is easy: they choose to work, no matter the personal sacrifice, financial or otherwise. Many dedicated theatre people would work for free, if they had to, just to have the opportunity to do whatever it is they do. Theatre producers knows this, of course, and some exploit it.

Customer satisfaction—audience approval—is measured at the box office. The number of tickets sold is a very reliable indicator of the success or failure, financial *and* artistic, of any theatrical endeavor. Few theatrical productions can afford to offer free admission. Even those that do must provide some level of audience (customer) satisfaction to remain in existence for any appreciable length of time. A successful theatre requires an audience. No audience, no theatre.

Management Skills

As a director, you are called upon to "manage" the various aspects of your production. You have day-to-day supervision of the many elements of the production over which you exert direct control—cast and crew, design staff, budget, scheduling, and so on. You will be required to make many decisions, often under severe time constraints and on the basis of precious little substantive, objective information. More often than not you will be flying by the seat of your pants, relying on experience, training, and a highly developed intuitive sense to see you through. Having a repertoire of managerial skills to call on is essential.

NEGOTIATING

To one extent or another, every conceivable aspect of your responsibilities as a director involves negotiation. You will find that there is virtually no one with whom you do *not* negotiate at one time or another during the course of a production. You negotiate with the producer for the terms of your employment, with the business manager for your budget, with the designers, the technicians, and the actors for your concept of the play. You also "negotiate" with an audience, on an artistic and interpretive level.

Most negotiations involve compromise. Compromise forces you to use your imagination to create new ways of thinking, to devise new and inventive solutions to old problems, to overcome obstacles, and to meet daily challenges. There may be no money for the set, for example, but think of all the possibilities that a bare stage offers.

Your ability to compromise (or *appear* to compromise) for the good of the production is essential to your effectiveness as a director. You will likely never have the "perfect" situation—the perfect cast, the perfect theatre, the perfect set, *and* the perfect budget all at the same time, all in the same place. All your attempts to reach that level of perfection are accomplished though negotiation.

Understand, first, that the theatre is filled with extremely diverse personalities. In your dealings with theatre people, and with theatre businesspeople, it is essential that you separate the people from the problems. It will not serve your purpose to alienate those with whom you are working. You must somehow try to preserve the working relationship. Remember, it's the policies or a particular situation you want to change, not necessarily the people whose job it is to implement and enforce the policies. Attack the *problem,* not the *person.*

It will help you in your negotiations if you focus on common interests rather than on individual issues or often irreconcilable philosophical differences. In the theatre, we assume a common interest—that everyone involved with a production wants to put on a good show. You want to put on a good show for artistic reasons, as do the cast, designers, and crew. The producer wants to put on a good show, possibly for artistic reasons, but more likely for financial reasons. The common interest therefore is putting on a good show.

The demise of the 1993 Broadway production of *The Red Shoes* is an example of the absolute necessity of a clearly defined common purpose. Many members of the production company of *The Red Shoes,* from the producer on down, had their own, personal vision for the show, but they failed to share a common vision. From the time the rights for a musical version of the 1948 film were acquired in 1989, rival factions within the development team—the producer, two different directors, the composer, the author/lyricist, the choreographer, and the designers—were vying for control of the artistic direction of the production. The show finally opened on Broadway after over four highly contentious years of "development." The show had fifty-one previews (indicating some very serious production problems), and closed after only five performances, with the considerable loss to investors—nearly eight million dollars—making it one of the greatest financial disasters in Broadway history.

Whether or not *The Red Shoes* was an artistic success is moot. The show didn't make it. After the reviews—unmerciful pans— appeared in the New York papers, advance ticket sales fell to $20,000 a week for a show that required $400,000 a week to break even. For lack of a common vision, eight million dollars and the personal and professional efforts of countless people involved with the production were lost.

Once negotiations are underway and a common ground is agreed upon, the next step is to find and explore reasonable *alternatives* to arrive at a mutually acceptable solution or agreement. There is rarely only one way to solve a given problem or to meet a given challenge. Explore a wide range of possible solutions before deciding (or agreeing) on a remedy. When people enter into negotiations in the real world it is generally assumed that no one will be totally happy with an agreement but that no one will be totally unhappy with it either. Unhappy people breed discontent. Discontent can spread through a theatre company very quickly, and can undermine an entire production.

You needn't lower your standards or compromise your integrity or your principles solely for the sake of an agreement. Whenever you enter into negotiations, decide on your bottom line. Give yourself room to negotiate, however. If you go into negotiations with a hard line and an inflexible, chip-on-your-shoulder attitude, you are likely to come out of those negotiations holding little more than your hat.

There will be times when you reach an impasse, when compromise is not possible, when you feel it is necessary to walk away. Be sure you have explored every possible alternative before you walk out. Walking out is relatively easy to do. Walking back in may prove much more difficult, particularly if the negotiations were at all contentious.

An effective negotiation technique is to *rely on some relevant precedent* on which to base an agreement. This could take the form of past expenditures, the going market rate for an item or service, or some other standard by which your progress toward an agreement or solution can be measured.

When you want to short-circuit the "that's the way we've always done it" response that is the favorite of maddeningly conservative theatre managers, producers, and boards of trustees everywhere, it may be help to rely on a "higher authority"—to cite precedents from *outside* your organization, preferably from organizations higher up the theatre-producing ladder, either in terms of prestige or financial success. *They tried it at the Guthrie last season,* you might say, *and it worked for them.* Be prepared, however, for the standard response, *But we're not the Guthrie,* which is intended to stop the discussion cold. Simply respond, *No . . . but we could be.*

Understand that a single negotiating meeting may not solve a problem and that not all negotiations result in agreement. It is better to come back to a second meeting (or a third or a fourth) with additional information or fresh alternatives than to struggle through a single, marathon meeting just to reach an agreement. View each meeting as an exploration of alternatives, as part of a process (like a rehearsal), rather than an end in itself. Above all, don't give up. The end product, the solution, will arise of its own accord if you provide the proper foundation and actively pursue an agreement. In the theatre, as we well know, it is often perseverance that prevails, even over talent and experience.

Listen actively in meetings and negotiations. The politics of negotiations—*what* is being said, *how* it is being said, and *by whom*—are often as important as the substance. Also be very clear in presenting your ideas. Be sure what you are saying is the same thing others are hearing. Disagreement in negotiations often arises as much, possibly even more, from miscommunication as from differences of opinion or policy.

If your negotiations fail, what then? If your negotiations are for your employment, you will need to decide whether or not to accept the position under the offered conditions. If the negotiations concern budgetary matters or artistic considerations, you'll need to decide what you are willing to live with (or possibly live without). As with the negotiations themselves, you need to have your own alternatives for other courses of action if the negotiations fail to bring about desired or acceptable results.

Business people are very familiar with negotiation survival skills and use them almost daily, but artistic people rarely use them when dealing and negotiating with theatre business people. Make a point of learning them:

1. Keep it simple. Express your ideas clearly, in a simple, straight-forward, nonconfrontational way. Artistic fits of temperament

will do you no good, and will more than likely seriously alienate those with whom you are negotiating. Secure, confident, competent artists rarely, if ever, resort to emotional displays to accomplish their goals. They don't need them. Their work speaks for itself.

2. Structure your presentation. Come straight to the point. Learn to view your thoughts and ideas objectively, particularly if you are presenting your ideas to a predominately pragmatic rather than artistic group of people. Keep the problem clearly in focus. Your proposal should be able to stand on its own merits. Avoid insubstantial supporting points or emotional arguments.

3. Anticipate opposition. You should have some idea of the basic objections to your ideas and proposals before you enter into negotiations. Send up a trial balloon well in advance (even at the risk of revealing your ideas prematurely), so that you can gauge possible negative reactions to your ideas. Prepare to address any negative response. Occasionally, you will find yourself negotiating with obstinate, highly opinionated, and/or dogmatic people. When someone who is aggressive or belligerent confronts you with an uncompromising position or attempts to intimidate or manipulate you, simply sit quietly and say nothing. Do not respond in kind. Keep the disagreement under your control, in your ballpark. Stay in control of yourself, in control of the situation, and in control of the direction of the negotiations. In most instances, the aggressor will eventually feel (and look) foolish and will grope for something intelligent to say to fill the terrible silence and/or to save face. Pay close attention: what follows will very likely be a softening of position, a slight pulling back from an otherwise hard line. This will give you an opening that you can turn to your advantage. Remember, too, that aggressive behavior usually emanates from some force or influence outside the matter at hand. Try to discern the true intentions, the true agenda, of the aggressor. He may be trying to disarm you, intimidate you, or manipulate you. Look behind the words to the motivations.

4. *Explain* your ideas. *Support* your ideas. *Demonstrate* your ideas. *Discuss* your ideas. But never *justify* your ideas. Your ideas are their own reason for being. You needn't justify them to anyone. Your ideas deserve respect and consideration, and a proper forum for expression. Great ideas take many forms, and the greatness of an idea is not always apparent at first glance. Ideas are to be encouraged and explored. Be sure that your ideas

receive a full and respectful hearing in an environment that is conducive to rational, reasonable discussion. Expect respect. If you don't get it, look elsewhere.

5. Take some "sacrificial lambs" with you into your negotiations. In other words, have a few relatively unimportant or expendable items that you can bargain away in order to protect the most important elements of your proposal. This is a standard real-world negotiating technique that works remarkably well, even though everyone knows that everyone else is doing it. It's part of the game.

6. Be flexible. You will elicit greater cooperation if you give the impression that you are open to other ideas, particularly from those who oppose or criticize *your* ideas. The risks associated with a take-it-or-leave-it approach are far greater than those of a more realistic and balanced approach in which there is room for give and take. The take-it-or-leave-it approach will fail far more often than it will succeed.

7. Whenever possible, incorporate opposition *into* your proposal. Blend reasonable objections into your ideas so that the finished proposal, the potential agreement or solution, resembles a common effort. Again, always give the *impression* of fostering an atmosphere of cooperation based on common interests and objectives, even in those rare instances when you are relentlessly and single-mindedly pursuing an objective about which you will tolerate no opposition or entertain no compromise.

8. Know your bottom line, and stick to it. Incorporate expendable items (your sacrificial lambs) into your proposal, and use them, but stop short of giving away the store for the sake of an agreement. Rather than seriously weaken your proposal by incorporating endless suggestions or modifications, offer to withdraw the proposal to reconsider it, restructure it, and resubmit it.

9. Be prepared to succeed. If your proposal is accepted, then what? Are you prepared to deliver? Are you prepared to assume responsibility for your proposal and implement it at the earliest opportunity? Worse than having a proposal rejected is having it accepted and then being unable to deliver what you've promised.

10. Be prepared to fail. Negotiations can go either way. What will you do if negotiations fail? Do you have alternative courses of action if your proposal is denied? Have you left yourself any room for further negotiations? Is there any possibility of reworking your proposal and presenting the "new and improved" version later? Have you got another job lined up, just in case things go badly for you? Be prepared to move on.

If negotiations do fail and you still feel very strongly about your position, remember the words of Davy Crockett: "Be sure you're right, then go ahead." You will find that if you carefully analyze a problem or a troublesome situation, and dedicate your considerable creative powers to resolving it, you will be right more often than you will be wrong. Being wrong could cost you your job, of course, but it's a chance that is often worth taking in the name of artistic, professional, and personal integrity.

Remember, too, the words of Davy Alberts: "It's easier to beg forgiveness than to beg permission." Do what you think is right. Don't *ask* if you can do it; just *do* it. If your plan fails, plead ignorance, stress, overwork, time constraints, or simply apologize, accept responsibility for the situation, and let the chips fall where they may. If your risk taking succeeds, accept the accolades, but don't let success go to your head. You were lucky this time. Your plan could just have easily failed.

To summarize negotiation:

- Separate the *people* from the *problem.* Avoid dealing in personalities.
- Focus on *common interests.* Establish a common ground.
- Explore *alternatives.* Give yourself room to maneuver.
- Keep lines of *communication* open. Listen. Learn.
- Be *flexible.* Be open to other ideas, opinions, and other possible solutions to a problem. Have alternatives if agreement is not possible.
- Think of negotiations as a *process*, not a *product.*

PLANNING

A director needs to be able to organize the diverse elements of the production into a focused, cohesive common endeavor and to project the consequences of actions and decisions well into the future. Organizational skills encompass not only the director's primary consideration—providing for the artistic unity of the production—but also the more pragmatic elements of day-to-day operations—scheduling meetings and rehearsals, managing the cast, organizing the technical elements of the production, and so on.

Ideally, a director should be prepared for any possibility, any opportunity, any disaster. In every production, however, something always happens that has never happened before, something totally outside the director's experience or awareness and for which he cannot be prepared. How you handle these little "somethings" will depend to a great extent on your skills in other management areas.

It is assumed that as a director, as a theatre artist, your creative thinking is highly developed. Directors have wonderfully creative ideas. When faced with a problem in implementing those ideas, however, many artists are at a loss.

Creative thinking is imaginative. The scope of the imaginative process is unlimited and unrestrained. In contrast, problem solving is pragmatic and reality based and takes place in a fixed, often quite limited environment. It is no wonder that many artists lack real-world problem-solving abilities. Practical, pragmatic problem solving is antithetical to an artist's way of thinking. Nevertheless, as a director you must maintain a delicate balance between your creative skills—the ability to think great thoughts—and your more pragmatic, problem-solving skills—the ability to implement those great thoughts effectively in the production process.

Creative problem solving requires an ability to recognize problems *and* opportunities and to *anticipate* problems and opportunities, in order to avoid or minimize the problems and maximize the opportunities. Being aware of a problem or opportunity is only half the process, of course; deciding what to do about it is the other half. You must also be prepared to reconcile your imaginative flights of fancy with the down-to-earth realization that you will not be able to implement all the wonderful and creative ideas that emanate from your incredibly fertile imagination. Usually, the budget won't allow it.

ASSIGNING PRIORITIES

A director needs to keep things in proper perspective, to pursue goals and objectives efficiently and effectively, and to function within clearly defined limitations and expectations. You are being entrusted with a precious commodity, a theatrical production; if you accept that responsibility, it is up to you to live up to the terms of your agreement regarding the production and the priorities and expectations of the producing organization as well.

The importance of the bottom line, in terms of the business of the theatre, has already been explained. Assigning priorities implies an ability to pursue the elements of the production in the proper order and in a manner that supports that bottom line.

Sometimes, for one reason or another, the bottom line is not clearly defined. There may be a problem with finances, for instance, or the organization may be undergoing change. The theatre management may simply be inept. Under those circumstances, it's best to take a conservative approach, and proceed accordingly until you have more specific information.

Generally, the basic elements of a production have an inherent priority. One thing usually leads to another, in a fairly predictable cause-and-effect way. It's only when there is a problem with the cause or the effect that priorities are called into question or brought more clearly into focus. Then, too, because of the ongoing cause-and-effect relationship of one element to another, there is never just *one* problem. Each problem leads to another problem.

Problems that arise while you are preparing for a theatrical production are complicated by inherent, sometimes inviolable, time factors. Certain things must be done by certain times. When those certain things *can't* be done by certain times or when completing one thing interferes with completing another thing, then priorities become very important. A clear set of priorities, encompassing as many areas of the production as possible, will help alleviate many problems. Each production is different, however, and priorities that serve one production may not serve another, so priorities must be redefined and negotiated for each situation.

RECOGNIZING QUALITY

A director must be able to recognize and encourage good work. First, you have to know what good work *is.* You may know good acting when you see it, and how to encourage it from your cast. Are you as knowledgeable about good work in the design and technical areas of your production? If you don't know what "good" is, technically speaking, how will you know it when you see it? How can you encourage it if you don't know what it is you're encouraging designers and technicians to do?

Encouraging good work is often a matter of reinforcing what already exists—one's self-respect and pride in one's work—conveying a true appreciation for a job well done, and reiterating that that work is important to the production. To recognize the work, praise it, and encourage continued good work takes only a few seconds, and your comments will be appreciated and well rewarded.

MANAGING FINANCES

Managing other people's money is a skill significantly different from managing your own money.

Every production has a budget, whether it's "no budget to speak of" for a community theatre production or a multimillion dollar budget for a Broadway show. You will likely have little or nothing to say about budgetary matters. By the time you are told the budget for your production, it will probably be too late to do anything about it. Protest a little, if it suits your purpose, but don't lose any sleep over it, and don't expect the budget to change to any substantial degree just because you don't like it. Make a few comments to the effect that you don't know how you can possibly do the kind of production they expect on that kind of money, but you'll try. Then, when you pull it off, you'll be invited to direct another show next season.

If you should be lucky enough to be consulted on the budget for a production, always, always, *always* inflate your requests by an amount equal to the organization's usual budgetary reductions. In other words, if most budget requests seem to be reduced by 20 percent, ask for 20 percent more than you need. If you ask for exactly what you think you need, you may end up with 20 percent less than you need, which could be disastrous. This artificial budgetary inflation may seem deceptive. It is. Nevertheless, it is very common and very necessary. It's also part of the game. Few members of the budget committee will be deceived by the ploy, so you can still sleep nights knowing that you've done the best you can to advocate for your production.

Common wisdom dictates that you never, ever come in under budget. (If you keep that up, they'll soon expect you to do a show for next to nothing!) Spend the money that you are allotted. Stretch the limits of your budget as far as you can. You'll be in a much better position to argue for more money for the next production if you can show that it took such-and-such an amount for the same item in the last production, and allowing for inflation, you should expect such-and-such an amount for the next production.

Nonetheless, you may decide to spurn common wisdom and come in under budget. It may be a matter of pride, or you may wish to promote goodwill in your organization on your own behalf so that when the artistic staff is hired for the next production, you'll be on it. There is nothing intrinsically wrong with coming in under budget. Just don't short the production to serve your personal ambitions. If you plan to come in 10 percent under budget, inflate your requests by that extra 10 percent.

An interesting distinction between a professional production company and an amateur organization is the role of the producer. In a professional company, the producer, as the employer of everyone associated with the production, wields considerable individual and organizational power. He draws from a wide and very competitive pool of actors, directors, designers, and technicians, and can demand a high level of competence and loyalty from the people he hires. He can also exert substantial pressure in all areas of the production.

The amateur producer (or an administrative representative of an amateur producing organization) wields no such power. In an amateur company, the producer serves as a coordinator rather than an employer. It is the producer's responsibility in an amateur organization to work *with* the artistic staff, to help facilitate their objectives for the production, rather than mandate how things should be done.

The amateur producer does, however, hold the purse strings, in the same way a professional producer does. In either organization, the producer can authorize or withhold expenditures in any production area. In an amateur theatre, however, the budget is likely to be considerably more inflexible than in a professional company. There is a limited amount of money for the show, and any changes to the budget must be approved by the administrative body of the theatre.

Your job, your responsibility, no matter what the budgetary limitations, is to manage and direct the best possible production that you can with the resources at hand. Remember that all you really need to put on a play are "two planks and a passion," and that the two planks are optional. Planks cost money, but passion is free. Use all the passion you can find, and the rest will take care of itself.

MANAGING PEOPLE

The director needs to put the right people in the right jobs and allow them the freedom to pursue their art and craft to the best of their ability.

Naturally, you'll want to hire the best people you can for the job (within the available budget). And if your staff has already been assigned, with or without your advice and consent, you will nevertheless do the best you can with what you've got.

Sometimes it serves a production well if the people you "cast" as your design and technical staff have to do a little stretching in their roles. Theatre people love a challenge. Even more, they enjoy meeting a challenge and exceeding expectations. There are times, of course, when only a seasoned, experienced professional will do. At other times, providing a person with a challenge may be just the incentive he or she needs to one day become the seasoned, experienced professional you seek.

Figure 1–1 is a basic flowchart of an amateur play-producing organization. Your organization may or may not be represented by this chart. (In fact, you may never work in the type of organization represented by this chart.) The chart depicts an ideal situation in which there is one person who is responsible for each major undertaking associated with the production. In some instances, particularly in small organizations and some educational theatres, one person may serve in many capacities. The set designer may also design the costumes and/or the lighting and sound. The stage manager may serve

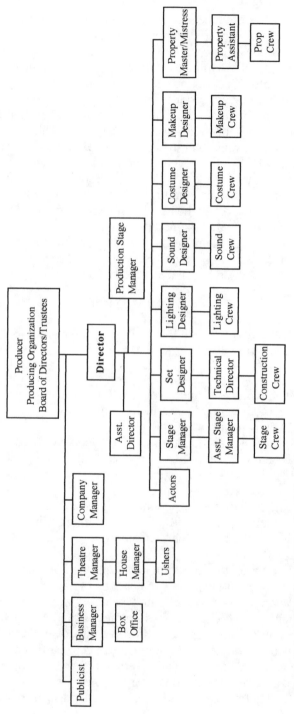

Figure 1–1. Theatre Organization Chart for a Play

as the props person. The producer may also be the director. The variations are endless. Each organization is unique. The smaller the organization, the more hats each member of the organization will wear. No matter the number of people, however, the number of hats remains the same. Somebody has got to be responsible for each of the essential functions of the organization.

Make it your responsibility to know who each person is, understand what each person does, what the areas of responsibility are, who her or his supervisor is (or should be), and all other pertinent and relevant information. You will meet some of these people only rarely. Others you will see daily, sometimes hourly. You will nevertheless communicate with every one of them, in one way or another, at some time during your tenure. It's important that you know *what* your organization is doing, *how* it's done, and *who* does it. It's a matter of self-preservation, if nothing else. Knowledge, as we all know (or will soon discover), is power. The more you know about what is going on around you, the less likely you will be caught unawares should matters take a turn for the worse. You will also be in a position to take full advantage of any opportunities that may arise that could be beneficial to the production.

One other thought. Note *your* position in the organizational hierarchy. There are people over whom you exert little or no direct control, such as the business manager, who can nevertheless influence various aspects of your production to a sometimes considerable extent.

Training ■ As a director you are also a teacher. You continually train and retrain your actors in rehearsal and encourage them to perform to their abilities, even exceed them. You constantly direct and redirect activity in every aspect of the production. At times, you may also be called upon to do more formal teaching, such as training the box office personnel or the front-of-house staff.

You will find that you teach as much by example as by direct instruction. You can expect, for instance, that the behavior of your cast and crew will be a reflection of your own behavior. Your "students" will do what you do. If you appear for rehearsals ill prepared, so will they. If you encourage them, by your example, to be cheerful and optimistic, well prepared, and respectful of one another, that is how they will behave. Expect that your cast and crew will do what you *do*, not necessarily what you *say*.

Also be aware that you wield considerable influence over everyone connected with your production, sometimes more influence than you can imagine or anticipate. What you teach them can have a significant effect on their personal and professional lives. You can literally change a person's life, for better or worse, within the context of a single production, possibly within a single rehearsal. It is an awesome responsibility, but one you must learn to accept when you direct a show.

Politics   ■   We encounter political pressures and politically related, politically motivated, and politically expedient decisions in almost every aspect of our lives. Much as we wish it were otherwise, the theatre is no different. Inherent in every aspect of your responsibility as director is the necessity to interact effectively with others at all levels within the organization to ensure the best possible production. You must do this within the limitations imposed by the producing organization, while maintaining some semblance of personal and artistic integrity. It's not easy.

Nothing in the theatre is ever as it appears. The impenetrable castle wall is really a painted canvas flat. The dead body gets up and walks off the stage after the curtain falls. Deception, in the positive sense, is the name of the game. Unfortunately, not everyone who works in the theatre understands that the deception should end at the footlights.

In the rarefied atmosphere of the theatre, emotions, motivations, and ambitions are all magnified as a matter of course. Learn to be sensitive to the people around you and to the reality of a situation. Be honest and straightforward in your dealings with others, and expect them to be honest and straightforward with you. If, however, things are not as they should be or not as they seem, if they seem too good to be true, or if you feel that you are not being treated fairly, look into it.

Try to ascertain the power behind the throne. Do the people on the board of directors wield equal power, or is there a noticeable concentration of power in one person or a small group? Is there a principal benefactor who expects certain considerations? Does a lifelong theatre patron have a disproportionate influence over the choice of plays, actors, directors, and designers?

In any event, avoid getting caught up in petty squabbles, interdepartmental rivalries, and similar contretemps unless the situation has a negative effect on your production. Be sensitive to any subtle pressures from established members of the organization, and be wary of any unreasonable or overly emotional response to your chosen path for a production. Be aware, also, of any problems or conflicts that arise within the acting company or the design/technical staff that seem to emanate from outside the rehearsal hall and design studio. Often these problems are simply the result of personalities in conflict, but sometimes the dissatisfaction being expressed is coming from elsewhere and is being channeled, knowingly or unknowingly, through the cast, crew, and staff.

Some directors feel that conflict is necessary, even essential, to the creative process and to the production of "good art," so they encourage a certain amount of unrest within the production community. Certainly, conflict and controversy may surround art, or arise from it, but it is rarely a necessary, intrinsic, or essential element of the art itself. The artistic unity of a theatrical production depends on a commonality of mind, body, and spirit of all involved and on a shared commitment that transcends individual ego or ambition.

Socializing ■ There may be times when you will be invited to mix and mingle with the local gentry, to chat up a wealthy benefactor, or to appear at a social function that may serve to benefit you or the producing organization in some way. You may consider these events an imposition. You may consider them a waste of time. You may even consider them demeaning. You will have to determine for yourself the relative worth to your career and to the organization of an occasional foray into the social sphere.

If you are socially adept and don't mind the occasional imposition on your time, these occasions can be beneficial to you and to your organization. Remember, however, that you do have work to do, and that nothing must interfere with your responsibilities. It is relatively easy to get caught up in the social whirl and to neglect the production.

In summary, effective management is the result of five basic skills, from which all other management skills emanate:

1. Effective directors are aware of and sensitive to the limitations imposed on the theatrical production by the script and by the producing organization. They also realize that there is no single right way to accomplish their goals for the production and that there are no universal laws governing the solutions to the many problems that arise during the preparation of a theatrical production. What works in one situation may not work in another. There are only specific and very particular needs that must be met within specific limitations, and those needs must be determined case by case.

2. Effective directors know what resources are available and how to use those resources to the production's best advantage. It is the director's responsibility to accomplish as much as possible with the available resources within the allotted time.

3. Effective directors keep an eye to the future and don't become so immersed in day-to-day matters that they lose sight of their goal. The director's concept and vision is the driving force behind the production. Good directors concentrate their efforts, and the efforts of everyone connected with the production, toward reaching and fulfilling that goal.

4. Effective directors know that a theatrical production continually changes and evolves, from the initial concept all the way through opening night and even beyond. Effective directors know and accept that uncertainty is an integral part of every production. They know they cannot anticipate all circumstances or plan for every eventuality. They are flexible and adaptable, open to change, and therefore prepared to address problems and able to capitalize on any opportunities that arise along the way.

5. Effective directors can create and foster a sense of urgency and excitement. They infuse the production with their own energy and enthusiasm and inspire in others a passionate commitment to achieving artistic excellence.

It seems, at times, that the least difficult part of being a director is directing. Directing may certainly seem to consume the least time and energy, create the fewest frustrations, and be the most fulfilling part of the endeavor. Nevertheless, those directors who can maintain the delicate balance between artistic and managerial responsibilities within the highly social and politicized environment of a theatrical production company are generally the most productive and the most successful.

The Director's Alter Ego

Your stage manager is the most important member of your production staff. He supervises the cast and all backstage crews throughout the production process—rehearsals and performances. He is the liaison between you and the cast and between you and the design and technical personnel. Frequently, he will be the only person who is in contact with every member of the cast, design staff, technical staff, and crew. Above all, the stage manager is the person whose primary responsibility is to expedite your artistic and administrative wishes and to maintain your vision for the production.

It is generally accepted that the stage manager is in charge of everything. (At times, it will seem as if the stage manager is in charge of you as well.) There is no definitive list of the stage manager's responsibilities for the simple reason that no two productions or producing organizations are the same. There are, however, some general guidelines:

1. He supervises all rehearsals and all performances.
2. He assembles and maintains a prompt book containing all information necessary to run the production efficiently in rehearsals and in performance.
3. He is the liaison between the director and the cast, between the director and the designers, and between the director and the heads of all departments.
4. He expedites the artistic intentions of the director in all areas of the production.
5. He maintains all production records.
6. He enforces and maintains discipline throughout the production company.

It is vital to your production, as well as to your mental health, to choose your stage manager well. Your stage manager must be extraordinarily dedicated. He will be expected to prepare for and attend every rehearsal and every meeting, supervise all backstage activities, and oversee the efficient running of every aspect of the production. He must be highly organized, efficient, tactful, self-disciplined, self-motivated, dependable, trustworthy, and knowledgeable in all areas of production. He must be a good manager and an effective leader. He must accept and, when necessary, assume responsibility for any aspect of the production that the situation requires. He must be unobtrusive but ever present. He must be firm but fair in all dealings with others at every level of the production. He must be highly adept at people skills: a good listener, a trusted confidant, and a hand-holder extraordinaire.

You will consult with your stage manager on every area of the production. Your stage manager will prove invaluable as a source of information and guidance regarding the theatre organization, the production, your cast and crew, designers, and administrative procedures and personnel. He will also serve as the voice of reason in times of stress or adversity or when you firmly believe that certain members of the production company have outlived their usefulness on this earth. Delegate as much responsibility to your stage manager as you possibly can and empower him to do what's necessary for the good of the production.

In some situations, you may not be able to choose the stage manager for your production yourself. This is not necessarily detrimental to you or to the production. If the person assigned is a long-standing member of the producing organization, it is likely that he has served capably in the past and will do so for you as well. Incompetent stage managers do not enjoy long careers. Welcome the stage manager to your heart as your would had you chosen him yourself. As with other assigned personnel, make the best of whom you've got.

A stage manager can help make or break a career. At the very least, a competent stage manager makes your job as director considerably easier. A more-than-competent stage manager can help you make it to the top of your profession. You would be well advised to treat your stage manager with the utmost respect and consideration. Support your stage manager in all his endeavors. Make sure your stage manager knows he is greatly appreciated and that everything he does is vital to the smooth running of the production.

The Director's Artistic Responsibilities

The director is solely responsible for the artistic *unity* of the production. The sense of unity the director is attempting to create *in advance* of opening night is something that can only be viewed *in retrospect.* That is to say, the unity of any work of art can be assessed only after the event has been experienced. It is a paradox, but one that directors have learned to live with and to accommodate in their work. To ponder the paradox is to invite madness. A director proceeds through the rehearsal period "as if" he knows what the result of the work will be. In truth, the director may have little or no idea of what's going to happen, ultimately, to the production. It's not a science, after all. It's an art. Art has a right to be paradoxical and unpredictable.

This unity is based to a great extent on the director's overall *concept,* or vision, for the production. The concept for the production is derived from the director's assessment of the predominant elements of the play—some combination of plot, character, theme, language, spectacle (or in the case of Shakespeare, all the above). It is the director's determination of the "world of the play," the metaphor to use, and any other goals or objectives for the production. The director must view the production in its entirety and develop a concept that projects his vision.

For the resulting production to be a unified and powerful work of art, the director's concept must be clear, bold, challenging, and comprehensive. It must be *clear* enough for every member of the production to understand it. It must be *bold* enough to create excitement and invite active participation. It must be *challenging* enough to sustain interest throughout the production process. It must be *comprehensive* enough to encompass every aspect of the production—staging, design, style, interpretation—and it must address general as well as specific elements of each area. The director's concept must provide the guiding principles for the synthesis of all the skills and abilities of everyone involved with the production, and it must inspire the creative artistry and personal and professional commitment necessary to sustain it.

Once the concept has been determined, the director must ensure its realization by every individual involved with the production and through every means available. Easier said than done, as any experienced director will testify.

Prerehearsal Organization | 2

D uring prerehearsal organization (or preproduction planning), one answers a seemingly never-ending stream of questions. What play shall we produce? Will the audience want to come to see it? How much will it cost? Who will design it? What are the performance dates? Can we cast it? It is only when all these decisions have been made, when all the questions have been answered, that preproduction planning ends and the production process begins.

There is a considerable range and variety of artistic and logistical tasks that the director must undertake well in advance of the rehearsal period. These tasks include selecting the play, preparing the script for rehearsals, making staff and design choices, planning the schedule, meeting with production personnel, and organizing and scheduling rehearsals.

Many artistic elements of a production are happy accidents that occur when creative directors, designers, and actors are brought together and encouraged to explore and grow within a supportive, empowering, and reinforcing environment. There are few, if any, happy accidents in the management of a production, however. It takes organizational skill, experience, and hard work.

Overview

The play production process falls into four main phases, or related groups of activities, as outlined below (these phases also apply to the production of a musical):

1. *PREPARATION*
    Play selection
    Scheduling
    Staffing
    Concept
    Design
    Casting

2. *IMPLEMENTATION*
    Rehearsals (orchestra as well, if a musical production)
    Construction (set, costumes, props)
    Technical preparations and implementation (lighting, sound, special effects)

3. *PRODUCTION*
    Performances
    Midrun changes (if any)

4. *POSTPRODUCTION*
    Evaluation (possibly as part of the preparatory phase of the next production)

Think of the process of producing a play as you would the development of a play itself—exposition, complications, conflict, climax, and resolution (or *denouement,* for the more learned among us). The "exposition" is prerehearsal planning. "Complications" and "conflict" most often occur in the implementation phase, during rehearsals, construction, and technical preparations. (It is here the greatest challenges invariably arise.) The "climax" is the opening night and the run of the show. The "resolution" is the postproduction evaluation—all the loose ends (if any) are tied up, the money (if any) is counted, the moral (if any) is learned, the dead bodies (if any) are removed from the stage, and the wounded (always a few) are treated. *Fini.*

This chapter and the next two examine each of the essential elements of the four production phases. In Chapter 5, these basic principles are applied to the production of a musical.

Play Selection

First, you have to "choose" a play. Rarely will this be a totally free choice. There are always "other considerations." There may be serious, even severe restrictions. You may have to submit your play choices to another person or group of people—the producer, a play selection committee, or a board of directors—for approval.

Well in advance, ask for a copy of the organization's mission statement, by-laws, or rules and regulations, which should contain information about organizational structure, play selection criteria, fund allocations, and other considerations, including casting preferences—all of which you need to know and fully understand before you begin the play selection process.

Work with plays that fall within your parameters or those previously determined for you by the producing organization—type of play, period in which the play is set, and cast size, for instance. Every director, even a novice, very likely keeps a list of Plays I've Always Wanted to Direct. Begin with that list. Augment it with suggestions from colleagues and other directors whose knowledge and experience you respect. Also review play catalogs and play lists for interesting possibilities.

Once you have a working list of about eight or ten plays that conform to your (or the organization's) basic requirements, consider each play relative to the following guidelines. (These play selection criteria are summarized in the checklist in Figure 2–1.)

AVAILABILITY

It is only common sense to ascertain whether or not the production rights to a play are available before you invest any time and effort exploring the possibilities of directing it. Unless the play is in the public domain—generally, plays written before 1900 and those no longer under copyright—you will need to apply to the author's agent, who is in most cases also the publisher of the acting edition of the play, for production rights. A quick phone call will tell you whether the play is available for production in your area and by your organization and what the royalties are, if any (see "Budget," page 31).

Some modern plays and the more recent Broadway successes may not be available. Play publishers and agencies don't do this just to annoy you, but to protect the playwright's interests, along with their own. Plays are sometimes unavailable for amateur production because a professional theatre in the area is doing the play, a national tour is coming to town, or a movie of the play is being released. On the other hand, if you notice that everybody in your area seems to be doing such-and-so play but you can't get the rights, it's because everybody is already *doing* it. Once agents and publishers feel that the market for a play in your area is saturated, they will limit or withdraw the production rights for that play for a time.

This is not a problem with plays in the public domain. Just because a play is available, however, is not enough reason to consider directing it. In order to protect your own interests, research any recent local and regional productions of the play. Your potential audience may be satiated with productions of *Romeo and Juliet, Tartuffe,* or *The Way of the World.* Depending on the relative mobility of your audience, consider amateur productions within an hour's travel time of your theatre and professional productions within two hours or more hours of travel time, particularly if you are near a major metropolitan area.

ACTING POOL

Can the available acting talent meet the demands of the script? What is the *age range* of the characters in the play relative to the range of ages available in your talent pool? What *range of experience and skill* will be required of your actors? A certain amount of stretch is acceptable, even encouraged, as long as the stretch is reasonable. What is the *cast size*? Can you fill all the roles with competent actors? In amateur organizations other than those in educational theatre, you will likely have difficulty casting more than eight or ten roles, not because there aren't enough actors available but because the level of talent and ability often drops precipitously after the first half dozen roles have been filled. Therefore, in most circumstances, it is better to choose a small-cast show for community theatres and similar amateur organizations. Certainly there are exceptional community theatre organizations with a wide range of acting talent from which to audition a large-cast show. For the most part, however, you should choose a play you *know* you can cast rather than one you have serious doubts about.

AUDIENCE

Who is your audience for this play? What is the relative age range of your potential audience members? What are their social and cultural backgrounds, their occupations, and their educational levels? The less sophisticated your audience, relatively speaking, the more they will enjoy plays that are strong on character, plot, and spectacle. The more sophisticated your audience, the more they will appreciate original ideas and the playwright's use of language. That doesn't mean that the less sophisticated audience deserves only shallow, meaningless melodramas, mind-numbingly loud music, and eye-popping special effects. Quite the contrary. The less sophisticated audience appreciates Shakespeare and O'Neill just as much as the more sophisticated audience does, for the simple reason that these playwrights know how to tell a good story with strong characters. A good story with strong characters is interesting and appealing to *any* audience.

Ask yourself, *Will the audience that regularly attends productions at this theatre come to see this play?* This is not to say you should only give an audience what it wants. Our mission in the theatre (should we choose to accept it) extends beyond simple appeasement and entertainment. We should try, whenever we can, to uplift the audience, to challenge them, to enlighten them, to enrich their lives. Certainly there are many popular plays that do just that. There are also many lesser-known plays, no less entertaining, that fulfill your artistic mission and that may well suit your audience. First, however, you have to get them in the theatre, which isn't easy. An unfamiliar play must have something compelling about it that will draw an audience otherwise reluctant to move beyond the familiar. If you can stretch the usual play-selection limitations, by all means seek out those less familiar plays that will stimulate you, your production company, and your audience.

The challenge in an educational theatre, as opposed to an amateur community theatre or a professional company, is to balance the educational objectives of the theatre program with at least a little concern for audience appeal. In an educational institution in which the theatre activity is largely extracurricular, the emphasis will be on audience appeal—Will the audience come to see this play? In a theatre training program, greater importance will be placed on the educational value of the performance program—Will the students *learn* from doing this play?

You will find that most educational theatres present a season of plays over which to balance educational value with audience appeal, so that no one play needs to fulfill both the educational and audience appeal criteria. Nevertheless, if you find yourself directing in an educational situation, make the effort to find those plays that *do* serve the students and the audience. Your job will be made considerably easier.

FACILITIES

Can you produce the play with the available rehearsal, performance, and technical facilities?

- Your rehearsal space should be equal to or greater than the size of the performance space. It should be in a minimally trafficked area, away from extraneous noise and distractions, well lighted, well ventilated, and located near restrooms and a source of fresh water.

- Consider the match between play and performance space. Is the performance venue suitable for this play? An intimate, small-cast play will be swallowed up in a thousand-seat auditorium, whereas your planned production of the complete cycle of Shakespeare's history plays, with cannon *and* horses, might overwhelm all but the largest theatre space.
- Are the lighting and sound equipment adequate for the needs of the play? The actors must be seen and heard. Can you meet this basic requirement with the equipment on hand or will you need to buy or rent additional lighting and/or sound equipment?
- Can the sets and costumes be built in-house, or must they be rented? If built, space must be available to build them. If rented, space must be available to store them. Depending on your budget and on the play, you might consider using minimal sets and costumes. However, the available facilities still need to be able to accommodate a "minimal" production of the play being considered. Some theatre companies do not have the luxury of anything but a performance space, which would seem to limit your play choices severely. All is not lost, however. You may be able to rent a warehouse or other storage facility for the run of the show. (Many self-storage facilities have very reasonable month-to-month lease arrangements. You may also be able to arrange for free or reduced rental in exchange for tickets or an ad in the program. Put your business manager to work on that.)
- Does the play require special effects? If so, are facilities and equipment available to produce them at reasonable cost? Will the extraordinary effects you hope to achieve require additional insurance to protect the producing organization against the increased possibility of personal injury or the destruction of the theatre? Local fire laws are one of those limitations imposed on a production that offer very little room for negotiation and compromise. You may need to substitute lighting effects for fireworks: what effect does this have on your choice of play? Will projections serve just as well, or are you adamant about setting the theatre aglow, figuratively and literally?
- How does your technical staff feel about the play? Are they excited by the prospect of working on it, or would they rather walk barefoot through a bed of hot coals? Has any member of your technical staff worked on a production of this play before? If so, what can she tell you about the positive and negative technical

aspects of producing it? Consider well what you are told. The suggestions and advice of your technical staff are invaluable.

Try to determine as best you can the level of technical difficulty involved in mounting the production of each play under consideration. Determine, too, the level of design and technical expertise required. Designers and technicians also need to stretch and develop their skills. Be sure, however, that the stretch is reasonably attainable.

BUDGET

The budgetary considerations with which you should be most concerned, in terms of play selection, are royalties and technical costs. Royalties range from little or nothing for plays in the public domain to $50 or $60 per performance for an amateur production of a straight play to upward of $300 or $400 (sometimes considerably more) per performance for a musical. Consult your technical staff about the relative costs in each technical area for the plays that you are considering. Ask them for a ballpark figure, so you'll have some idea of the overall production costs for each play. Generally, you will find that your budget for technical items, including set and costumes, will be determined to a great extent by the following:

1. What you see is what there is.
2. If you want more, it's gonna cost ya.
3. There's no money. See #1.

If you've determined that your budget is sufficient to produce *any* play on your list, then it's a matter of considering the other guidelines in order to make a decision. If your budget is insufficient for one or more of the plays, you will need to delete it/them from your list, at least temporarily. You may be able to find some way to finesse the budget at a later date with some creative financing, but for now, put your time into the more viable options.

THE SEASON

In organizations that produce a season of plays, rather than an infrequent change of bill or a single long-running production, you will need to consider where and how your play will fit into the overall scheme. In some seasons there will be a mix of periods, styles, and genres. Another season may be devoted to one central theme, period, country, or even to one playwright—a full season of Shakespeare's plays comes readily to mind. There is no such thing as a "perfect season." What may be perfect for one theatre will prove disastrous for another. The best seasons conform to the highest artistic standards and offer the greatest overall audience appeal. As with most other aspects of theatrical life, the "perfect season" is a compromise between an ideal and reality.

If much of the season is already known, look closely for (or inquire about) common themes or other elements in common among the various plays. Also ask whether there is a traditional type or style of play that is usually performed in your particular slot. Is yours the comedy slot or the mystery/drama slot, for instance, or will the entire season be built around your choice of play? This last option is highly unlikely, but it happens occasionally that a well-known director is engaged to direct a play, and the season is chosen and balanced around the play she chooses to do.

If the rest of season is unknown or has yet to be determined and no specific criteria have been stipulated, then it may prove most advantageous for you to submit a range of periods and genres—a comedy, a drama, and a mystery, for instance. By all means submit your first choices, but be prepared with alternatives (possibly several) if your selections are rejected.

Also find out whether the producing organization has any expectations for the production. Are you supposed to make money with this play, or will this be the artistic success of the season—great reviews, critical acclaim, but limited audience appeal? Is this a loss leader—a costly, large-scale production designed primarily to fill the seats in anticipation of return customers? Or is this a cost-cutter—small cast, unit set, modern dress, preferably with considerable audience appeal?

Performance Dates

You may have little or no control over performance dates. It's not really your responsibility. The performance dates may influence your play choice, however.

Consider your performance dates in relation to national, regional, and local holidays and events of national interest. The fact that your play is scheduled at the same time as one of these holidays or other events is not necessarily detrimental. You can turn a potential liability into an opportunity. Look for possible tie-ins to activities or events that might generate audience interest and help increase attendance. You might also consider playing *against* a well-known event—a nationally televised football game, for instance—in order to offer an alternative to those who may be dissatisfied or disenchanted with the prospect of spending their entire afternoon and/or evening in front of the television set watching extraordinarily large men repeatedly crash into one another.

The Thanksgiving-Christmas-Hanukkah period is a good time for seasonally oriented plays (*A Christmas Carol, The Man Who Came to Dinner*). New Year's is actually a pretty good time of the year, particularly for upbeat productions and musical revues. People want to go out and have a good time. (They don't particularly want to have to *think*, though. They just want to be entertained.) Valentine's Day is a good opportunity for a tie-in for plays with a romantic theme (*Romeo and Juliet*). Easter/Passover often coincides with spring break or school vacations, and you may have difficulty filling the house for a serious drama, although a musical or a comedy might do quite well. Be aware, however, that it seems to be a tradition of long standing that every high school in America does a musical in the spring. The Fourth of July sometimes poses a problem, depending on what happens to the general population in your part of the country. If everyone heads for the seashore for the long holiday weekend, then maybe that's where you should be, too. If you're already at the seashore, or somewhere else where there is generally an influx of visitors, it might be to your advantage to offer them some topical theatrical diversion—*George M!* or *1776*, for instance, or any other patriotically oriented play or musical.

You will need to do some research to determine the effect of holidays and other events on previous attendance at your theatre. If you find the effect is usually detrimental, you can (1) try to change the performance dates, (2) try to schedule a play with considerable audience appeal to counteract the expected reduction in attendance, or (3) expect small audiences.

As in every instance noted above, it's important that you be aware of *all* the criteria imposed on your play selection process, even the most seemingly arbitrary and unartistic considerations, so that you can make an intelligent and informed decision.

THE DIRECTOR

As the director, you are the most important part of the play selection process. You need to ask yourself, first, if you are *capable* of directing the play—if you have the skill equal to its complexity—or if you just *want* to direct it. Certainly your desire and your willingness to direct a play are important factors to consider in choosing one play over another, but equally important is an honest assessment of your abilities and capabilities in relation to the play. Do you have experience in or a good working knowledge of the period and style of the play? Do you understand the characters' relationships and motivations? Are you in tune with the theme of the play? Can you do justice to what you believe are the playwright's intentions? It is vitally important to the success of your production that you answer yes to all these questions. These essential elements of your personal approach to directing a play cannot be acquired through on-the-job training.

Occasionally you will be asked to direct a play that has already been selected. All other considerations being equal, apply the same criteria to the already-chosen play as you would if you were choosing the play yourself. However, your enthusiasm for the project (or lack thereof) should be your overriding consideration. If the prospect of directing this play excites you, if it ignites your imagination, if you're enthusiastic about it, then do it. If the play engenders only a lukewarm response, or none at all, say no. You must *want* to direct the play.

MAKING THE CHOICE

There is no disgrace in making a selection from a list of small-cast, single-set, modern-dress, lights-up-lights-down, audience-appealing, low-budget plays. Experienced directors welcome the opportunity to direct "small" plays, particularly if they challenge the creative artistry of the actors, director, and designers.

The problem with a "big" show is that so much time and energy is spent on the bigness of the undertaking that little time is available to pursue creative flights of fancy, to experiment, sometimes even to think. A small play affords everyone connected with the project considerable opportunity to explore its artistic challenges. Imagine the difference in the potential levels of accomplishment between working through a three-hour rehearsal with two or three actors and working through the same rehearsal with a "cast of thousands." You cannot devote the same amount of time and energy per person with a large cast as you can with a small one. You cannot expect the same level of individual development. You can still reach the heights of artistic achievement you desire when directing a big show. More often, however, you will be exhausted from the attempt, and happy just to be alive by the time the show opens.

It's all a matter of priorities, personal as well as organizational. If the priorities dictate "bigness"—big cast, big set, big budget—then by all means choose from a list of "big" plays. You will likely encounter challenges to match. If, on the other hand, the priorities allow for a "small" play (and particularly if you are an inexperienced director), then choose the play that gives you and your actors and designers the greatest opportunity to develop your respective arts. Whenever possible, choose an artistic challenge over a project that requires sheer physical and mental endurance.

Availability
- [ ] Budget (royalty costs) and contract terms (restrictions on cutting the play, for example).
- [ ] Recent area performances.

Acting Pool
- [ ] Adequate number of actors to cover roles, sufficient age range, skills and experience.

Audience
- [ ] Demographics. Interests. Past successes.

Facilities
- [ ] Adequate and workable rehearsal, performance, and technical space.
- [ ] Technical support available for all aspects of production—set, costumes, lighting, sound, special effects (if any).
- [ ] Interest and enthusiasm for play among technical staff.
- [ ] Approximate cost of technical support to feed into budget considerations.

Budget
- [ ] Level of financial support beyond "two planks and a passion."

The Season
- [ ] Appropriate to season programming, if applicable, in terms of period, theme, genre, or other considerations.

Performance Dates
- [ ] Possible tie-ins to local, regional, national holidays or events, if appropriate or applicable.
- [ ] Liabilities regarding same.

The Director
- [ ] Sufficient skills and experience to direct the play.
- [ ] "Small" play vs. "big" play.
- [ ] Personal interest and enthusiasm.
- [ ] Understanding and empathy with characters and theme of the play.

Politics
- [ ] External influences, considerations, pressures regarding the choice of play.
- [ ] "Playing the game" to best effect.

Figure 2–1. Play Selection Checklist

If the usual procedure in your theatre is to submit your choice of play(s) to a play selection committee or other decision-making entity over which you may or may not have some influence, then hedge your bets. Don't submit only one play, and don't appear to favor one play over another. Choose two or possibly three plays that you can live with, and submit all of them to the committee. And remember, it's politically expedient to let the committee have the final say, since they then share the responsibility (and any potential liability) for the choice.

Even if you wield enough influence over members of the play selection committee to ensure your first choice, submit two or three choices anyway, if merely to maintain appearances. Let your friends on the committee lobby for your choice in your place. (Allow your supporters their dignity, at least, even if you've taken away their free will.) It's a civilized and respectful way for you to treat your colleagues. (Never flaunt your advantage, however. It's one of the surest ways of losing it.)

If the choice of plays is said to be yours alone, but really isn't, do not get caught in the trap of lobbying hard for one particular play only to have that choice rejected by those who have the power to choose the play and to enforce their choice. Submit two or three plays (again, the ones you can live with), and defer to the wisdom of the powers that be. Even if you are pressed hard for a first choice, don't tip your hand unless you're sure that voicing your opinion will not backfire. Try to make sure that the powers that be share the responsibility for the choice of play with you, thereby limiting your personal, professional, and political liability.

If the choice of play really and truly is yours alone (it rarely is), look closely at all the plays and weigh very carefully all the criteria. Bite the bullet, and choose the play that best fulfills the overall production criteria and about which you are most enthusiastic.

Preparing for Rehearsals

Once the play is chosen and you start preparing the script, scheduling rehearsals, and so on, keep in mind that no one connected with this production should know more about this play than you do—not the actors, not the designers, not the producer, not even the playwright. You must be the supreme authority. There is no way you can begin directing a play without becoming absolutely, totally, and intimately familiar with every aspect of it.

Learn all you can about the play, the playwright, the period in which the play was written, the period in which it is set, and any forces that may have exerted an influence on the play's genesis and development. Research the costumes of the period, the social attitudes of the time, and any other aspect of the play with which you are not completely familiar, and carefully review those aspects of the play with which you *are* familiar. Read reviews of past productions for subtle and not-so-subtle hints on potential problem areas and for audience reaction. Read promotional materials from other productions for some idea of what others considered important to emphasize.

Ideally, you need a minimum of eight weeks before rehearsals begin to become familiar with the script and assimilate all relevant information. If you are a last-minute hire or replacement, you will have considerably less time than that. No matter. You just have to do it in the time you have. It's an absolute necessity that you know all there is to know about this play. If directing were easy, anybody could do it!

PROMPT SCRIPT

A well-prepared prompt script will prove invaluable throughout the rehearsal process. The prompt script is the central location for all the information you will need during the next several weeks—your blocking, your concepts, ideas, thoughts, and inspirations, your notes on designs and other technical considerations, your research, and so on.

Once you've decided on a play and received a working copy of the script, prepare your prompt script. Since the prompt script will contain a great deal of information in addition to the script, get a three-inch loose-leaf binder. (Depending on the complexity of the production, you may fill more than one.) Use whatever format you choose to mount the script pages, and put the script in the binder. Add an extra blank page for your notes in front of every script page. Insert tabs for each scene, so you can quickly refer to any part of the script. In addition, include a copy of your master schedule, rehearsal schedule, and all technical schedules; cast lists; notes and memos to the designers, cast, and crews as they accumulate; and any other information relevant to the play or to the production that you may need to consult during the rehearsal period. If you like, use tabs to separate this material from the script. Also keep a separate reference section in your binder for your research materials.

Some general notes about prompt scripts:

1. Write in pencil. You will change your mind. Often.
2. Write neatly. Printing is recommended. There are few things more frustrating than being unable to read one's own writing,

particularly that supremely inspired bit of blocking that you scrib-
bled on the script at two o'clock this morning.

3. Keep your prompt script neat. Write blocking and other notes in
   the margins, rather than on the printed script and draw lines
   (preferably straight) from your margin notes to the relevant por-
   tions of the script.
4. Entrust your prompt script to no one, not even your most trusted
   colleague, friend, or relative. There will be information in your
   prompt script that cannot be re-created, replaced, or duplicated at
   any price. Limit the number of places that you take your script, or
   that you leave it—your home, your office, and the rehearsal hall
   ought to be sufficient. (If your office *is* your home, the odds of losing or misplacing the prompt script are reduced by one third.)

After the production has closed, some directors have their
prompt scripts bound as a book. This bound script usually contains
production photographs, reviews, feature articles, and so on, in addition to all the other material that has accumulated throughout the
production process. (If you drop a hint to the stage manager, the cast
may have your prompt script bound for you as a gift. Since the cast
is often at a loss about what to give the director as the traditional
"small token of appreciation," you might be doing everyone a favor.)

These bound copies serve little useful purpose, but they look
good on the shelf, particularly as they accumulate over the years, and
the programs and pictures they contain will "prompt" wonderful
memories. You can also consult your prompt script library when you
direct a play you've directed before or use it to impress prospective
employers or producers. For the most part, however, your bound
prompt script will gather dust until you pull it off the shelf to remi-
nisce about the good old days.

Cutting the Play

Put yourself in the playwright's shoes. If you had spent weeks,
months, even years sweating over each and every word, making sure
it was the exact right word, in the exact right place, for the exact right
effect, would you want someone to come along and change your
words, cut out a line here and there, change the order of scenes, perhaps chop out entire scenes altogether? Probably not.

On the other hand, as the director, you need to be able to mount
the most stageworthy production you can. There are very few plays
that couldn't do with a little judicious cutting—a word here or a line
there—particularly older plays in which there are archaic or obscure
references that are unfamiliar to a modern audience. With modern

plays, however, cutting or altering the text may be expressly forbidden by your production agreement, in which case you will be in violation of your contract and the play's copyright as well.

There are also local attitudes and moral standards to consider. You will need to decide whether the playwright's choice of words (and/or action) could offend members of your audience. Perhaps a change in phraseology is all that is needed to make the play more acceptable to audiences in your community. (Sometimes, however, "darn" or "heck" do not convey the effect the playwright had in mind in writing a particularly emotional scene.) This is not to encourage wholesale censoring. Choose a different play rather than destroy a play's integrity to appease local (usually self-appointed) guardians of good taste and morality.

If a play is worth doing, it is worth doing as near to the original script as possible and as near to the playwright's intentions as possible. Cut a modern or otherwise controlled script only with permission, and cut any other script only to improve the clarity of the plot, characters, or theme, and to make it more stageworthy.

Casting

Casting a play is one of the most important parts of the production process. You probably have a pretty good idea of *how* to assemble a cast, but for one reason or another you may have been disappointed with the results.

The creative process is, more often than not, simply a creative application of a logical process. Casting a play is no exception. What follows is an efficient and effective approach to casting a play, from planning the auditions through making the final choices. There is no inherently right or wrong way to manage the process, only the way that is most efficient and most appropriate in your situation.

The term *audition* can mean different things to different people. There are auditions, there are tryouts, and there are readings. There are prepared readings and there are cold readings. There are individual auditions and there are auditions involving a seemingly overwhelming number of people. Sometimes there are casting meetings or interviews where no auditioning, as such, seems to take place.

A *reading* implies a certain emphasis on the script, whereas an *audition* or *tryout* may encompass other activities, such as singing or dancing. Actors read for plays, for instance, and audition for musicals. For the most part, however, the terms *audition, tryout,* and *reading* are used interchangeably.

Call it what you like, but be sure to provide sufficient information far enough in advance of the auditions so that the prospective auditioner has some idea of what to expect. If a prepared audition piece is required or encouraged, mention that in the preaudition information. If any roles have already been cast, it is only fair to inform your auditioners of that, too, so they don't come prepared to read for a part that is no longer open.

If possible, provide scripts for the actors to read in advance, so they can become familiar with the play and with the range of characters. (Copies of the script may be signed out from the front office, if appropriate, or put on reserve at a local library.) Making the scripts available serves a dual purpose. The actors will be better prepared for the auditions if they are familiar with the play, and those who are ultimately cast in the play will have a head start on learning their lines.

A prevailing attitude in some organizations seems to be, *Let's just surprise the actors and see how well they cope.* Since few plays or musicals require this particular skill, asking the actors to jump through hoops to get cast is demeaning, at best. Cold readings, too, seem to serve little useful purpose, although the practice is used extensively. There are very few occasions when an actor is handed a brand-new script on opening night and pushed onstage. Many directors are adamant about including cold readings in auditions, and rely heavily on actors' abilities at cold readings in casting. These directors run the risk of casting the best readers rather than the best actors.

The overriding consideration in auditions is, or should be, to give the actors every opportunity to do the best they can. Some very fine actors do not read well in auditions but are perfectly fine in performance. Actors who are dyslexic are at a considerable disadvantage in a cold reading, although their disorder has no detrimental effect on their acting, singing, or dancing ability. If there is a reasonably level playing field, for which all auditioners are reasonably well prepared, you should be able to discern the relative strengths and weaknesses of those who audition for you.

PREAUDITION PREPARATION

Before holding auditions, you should determine what, *exactly,* you are looking for in the actor you intend to cast in each role. Make a list of available roles. Decide on the essential characteristics an actor should have in order to portray a role effectively and list them under the character name. Write down both general and specific guidelines: the relative age and overall physical appearance of each character, as well as vocal quality, interpretive ability, and any other characteristics that you feel are important. Do this for every role in the play, no matter how minor. This is a very important, since your choices will be made relative to these criteria. Keep the list close at hand during the auditions, and refer to it in relation to every auditioner.

During auditions, list under the character name every actor who fulfills or comes close to fulfilling your predetermined criteria for that role. (An actor may appear on more than one list, as they may be suitable for more than one role.) This will form the basis (perhaps the entirety) of your callback list. It will also greatly simplify the casting process.

Take the time during the auditions to write notes to yourself about the auditioners. You needn't write something about everyone, but you should make notes about those with the strongest potential. Trust your memory if you like, but you may forget something important that could affect the casting of the entire show. Avoid writing *while* people are auditioning, of course. There is nothing more disheartening to an auditioner than to look out into the house and see the top of the director's head while she scribbles away on her legal pad. There is ample time after each auditioner finishes to write down a few brief notes.

Casting notes should not be written on the audition form, which might be seen by others—those who may be compiling mailing lists for the theatre or otherwise just poking through the forms. Use three-by-five sticky notes instead. (Some directors prefer file cards, but those can become a jumble, particularly if there is a large turnout.) When the auditions are over and the casting complete, you can destroy the notes or retain those you wish to consult during future casting.

Many directors have devised their own shorthand—abbreviations or foreign words and phrases, for instance—to facilitate the process and to discourage deciphering by anyone other than themselves. If you employ this method, be sure you remember what all those abbreviations mean!

AUDITION FORMS

Every theatre organization seems to have a unique audition form. Most are inadequate. If the "standard" audition form is inadequate for *your* purpose, then change it. Ask for the information that you, as the director (or as a member of the casting committee), want and need to know. If name, address, phone, height, weight, and previous experience are insufficient, ask for more. If you are interested in additional performance skills the actors have, ask them for a list or provide a checklist. (A Casting Questionnaire, much like those used by professional casting agencies, is included as Appendix B. Amend it to suit your situation.) The audition form is a tool, and like any tool, it should be appropriate for the job.

"Will you accept any role?" may be phrased on the audition form in one of several ways—*For which role (or roles) are you auditioning?* or *Will you consider other roles?* or *Is there any role for which you would prefer not to be considered?* The bottom line is the same—some actors wish to be considered only for a specific role or roles. Some prefer to be considered only for lead and/or secondary roles. Others (very few) may wish to be considered only for minor roles, walk-ons, or a part in the chorus.

The reasons actors prefer a specific role or a limited range of roles are as varied as the actors. It may be a matter of pride or self-respect, time constraints, or some other real-world commitment. Some actors prefer not to commit their time and effort to anything less than a lead. Another actor may not be able to attend the three hours of rehearsal every night for eight weeks that a lead role requires. It is disconcerting to discover, after you've finally managed to cast the show, that one or more of your prospective cast members has indicated on her audition form that she would prefer not to be considered for the role in which you've cast her. It happens.

There are basically two ways to approach this situation. You can (1) take the actor at her word and consider her *only* for those roles in which she has expressed an interest or (2) consider the actor's wishes as a rough guideline and approach each role case by case. In the first instance, you risk not being able to cast this person at all, even for roles for which they may be ideally suited. In the second instance, you risk casting a person in a role that she may not wish to accept.

One way to limit this type of situation (perhaps even avoid it altogether) is to require more than a yes or no response to the acceptance/nonacceptance question. Some directors require (as is often done in educational organizations) that all auditioners sign a statement that they will accept whatever role is offered. This would seem to eliminate the problem, but, unfortunately, it doesn't. An actor is free to refuse a role, for whatever reason, and may well do so. The trouble is, you will not be aware of her refusal until after the cast list is posted.

A less risky (and less heavy-handed) approach is to pose the question on the audition form and to make sure the auditioner understands that by responding "no" she will be considered *only* for the roles she has indicated. If she is not cast in one of those roles, she will not be cast at all. An actor may still not accept a role, but the likelihood is lessened considerably. You might also provide a space on the audition form where the actor can write a brief explanation of the reasons she will or will not accept any role. The more information you have, the better you will be able to complete the casting process, with fewer complications.

The most reasonable approach to this sometimes troublesome situation is to confer privately with the actor. Explain the situation. Tell her you noticed that she was only interested in a particular role but that you would like to consider her for something else. If she agrees, fine. Otherwise, respect her wishes.

PHOTO AND RÉSUMÉ

Whether or not you require that actors supply a headshot (an eight-by-ten glossy head-and-shoulders photograph) and résumé is a matter of choice and of the tradition within the producing organization. For professional organizations, they are essential. Initial casting is often done by casting directors from headshots and résumés alone, with follow-up auditions for the chosen few.

In amateur organizations, the use of headshots is usually optional. Quite often, amateur actors cannot afford a professionally produced photograph. Since acting is not the amateur's life's work, they needn't be required to furnish a professional headshot for the occasional audition. You certainly wouldn't turn away an actor who provides one even when it is not required, and it would be discourteous to bar an actor from auditions just because she doesn't have a headshot.

In organizations that don't require a headshot, it's a good idea to take photos of the actors yourself, particularly if you are auditioning a large number of people or if you are not familiar with the talent pool. It's too easy to dismiss an actor simply because you don't remember what she looked like. You may be tossing away valuable talent. On the other hand, you may *mis*remember what an actor looked like and cast one actor thinking you are casting someone else, and be surprised by an unfamiliar face at the first read-through.

To take these audition photos, you will need an "instant" camera and a supply of self-developing film—plan for thirty or forty actors per roll of ten-print film. (It's wasteful and expensive to take a photo of only one actor per print.) As the actors arrive, have your stage manager (or an assistant) line up three or four of them side by side, take the photo, cut the picture apart, and then staple or otherwise attach the small photo of each actor to the front of the audition form or résumé. There you have it—"instant" recognition and no merry mix-ups.

Some theatre organizations videotape the auditioners, one at a time, just before they do their audition—they say their name and hello. This helps the director remember not only each auditioner's face but also his or her voice. The entire audition is not usually taped, as this may involve legal matters having to do with the use of copyrighted material. Then, too, a taped performance rarely compares favorably to a live one.

As for résumés, quite frankly, most of the information on them, even if true, is relatively meaningless. It may be helpful to know that the actor has had ten years of acting classes, five years of voice lessons, and seventeen years of ballet, but unless the teachers are very well known, little point is served. As for acting experience, you will see everything from a small, round lad, not yet twenty, fresh from his success as Hamlet to an ingenue who has played Polonius (in the all-female version) to a matronly type trying to pass herself off as Ophelia. No matter how impressive a résumé may be, it's still best to judge an actor's suitability for a role from what you see in front of you, not from what it says on a piece of paper.

WATCHERS VERSUS DOERS

Try to keep the number of observers to a minimum. It's an audition, after all, not a performance. You, the stage manager (and an assistant), the producer (or producer's representative), and the casting committee (if any) are the only people who need to be there. Add a few ushers to handle forms, photos, and résumés if a large turnout is expected. (For musical auditions, the music director and choreographer need to be added to the list.)

PRECASTING

Precasting is always worrisome. Generally speaking, make no commitments to actors before the auditions and resist as best you can any imposed or "suggested" casting that may filter down to you through the organization. Resist, too, the temptation to cover all your bases by intimating to an actor that she has a good chance for a role if she'll just show up for auditions. (What you mean by that, and what an actor perceives that you mean by that are often very different things.) It's important to keep your casting options open. You never know what new and exciting talent might appear at auditions. If you've already promised a particular role to another actor, you may have to pass on the newcomer or do some fancy dancing when you explain your casting decision to the actor who thought you had promised the role to her. All in all, consider the good of the production.

The overriding concern, particularly among amateur theatrical organizations, is whether or not precasting will limit the number and range of actors who will audition. If an actor knows that she no longer has a chance for a leading or featured role, will she simply write off the auditions and look elsewhere, or will she attend in hopes of getting a secondary or minor role?

Also, the other cast members may resent the precast actor, particularly if it is thought the person was not cast on the basis of talent alone. Actors usually have no problem with others of their number being precast *if* those so cast deserve being shown preferential treatment by reason of talent, experience, or celebrity. They *do* have a problem with actors who, for one reason or another, prove unworthy of their preferred status. This resentment will manifest itself in sometimes obvious, sometimes extremely subtle attempts to "disenfranchise" the offending party. Actors are imaginative and clever people who are in the business of expressing their innermost self. They will find some way to express their dissatisfaction with the situation.

If you must precast an actor, for whatever reason—contractual agreement, sheer talent, "star" status, training program, or politics—be sure the precasting is clearly stated in the preaudition announcements. At auditions, announce which roles have already been cast (although you needn't necessarily announce who has the parts), and, if at all possible, avoid having auditioners read those parts. This will help dispel the false hope that the auditioner will be able, somehow, to displace the precast actor from the role with an overwhelmingly powerful and compelling reading.

You may, however, consider auditioning understudies for precast roles. Be sure that auditioners understand very clearly that they are only being considered as understudies for the precast roles but that they will be given full consideration for other available roles. Just hope that the precast actors are not shown up in auditions and that they come through with the goods in rehearsals and performance.

UNDERSTUDIES

The problem with understudies is not so much whether or not to have them, which is a matter of individual or organizational preference, but how to assign them in a way that doesn't throw the entire production into total chaos when one actor is indisposed and another actor must be substituted.

Let's assume, for instance, that actor B is understudying actor A, and actor C is understudying actor B. When actor B takes actor A's role, and actor C takes actor B's role, who covers for actor C? The actors become entangled in an extended version of musical chairs, all precipitated by only one missing actor!

The potential for disarray is heightened in a small cast. If any of the major and secondary roles understudy each other, there could be considerable shifting of actors and roles, to the overall detriment of the production. It is therefore sometimes advisable to cast actors as understudies only, particularly for lead roles, and to ask an assistant stage manager or some other backstage person to cover the secondary and minor roles.

Being an understudy is a thankless job, particularly for "walking understudies," or standbys, who hold no other part in the play. Understudies dream of getting a shot at the big time, but it is a dream few ever realize. They may sit through every rehearsal and attend every performance, yet never set foot in front of the audience. That's life in the theatre.

Some directors reject the notion of understudies, preferring instead to trust the gods to protect them, as they protect all children and fools. Nevertheless, it is only prudent to have some sort of understudy arrangement, even an informal one, just in case. More than once, a director has been called upon to stand in for a missing actor. It's a sad and forlorn sight, indeed—the director wandering the stage, script in hand, mumbling to herself, trying to remember the blocking she herself created.

At the very least, a secondary player of each sex should be designated to cover the appropriate major roles, a minor player of each sex should be asked to cover secondary roles, and the stage manager or assistant stage manager should be prepared to cover minor roles and walk-ons.

Choose your understudies carefully. They will have to attend extra rehearsals, possibly learn two different sets of lines, and otherwise assume a considerably greater responsibility than being cast in a single role requires. Your understudies should be conscientious, trustworthy, and emotionally stable. Taking over a role on short notice can be very stressful. Be sure that your understudies can handle the pressure.

HOLDING AUDITIONS

As you may have experienced firsthand, there are several ways to manage the audition. If the audition consists entirely of prepared monologues, then it's a matter of organizing a schedule of the participants (a sign-up sheet or some other method) and progressing through the list. A callback list (or cast list) is posted within a day or two, and the rehearsals proceed. This is one of the most efficient ways to handle auditions, but it is the least effective means of auditioning and casting an amateur production.

The preparation of audition monologues, a staple of actor train-ing programs everywhere, is highly overrated. First, there are very few monologues, relatively speaking, in the dramatic literature. Most plays involve *dialogue*—character to character, not character to her-self. Second, a monologue gives the actor (and the casting director) a false sense of her actual abilities. Just because an actor can do a bang-up job of "I left no ring with her . . ." at an audition is no guar-antee she can sustain the role of Viola for the balance of the play, not to mention all that falling in love business and dressing up like a man. Last, the director has no frame of reference in which to evalu-ate the potential of the actor. How long, for instance, has the actor been preparing this monologue? Months, perhaps, or even years? How will the actor fare with new material after only a few weeks of rehearsal? What else can this actor do? Does this actor have any range? You can request that the actor prepare "two contrasting pieces," but the same questions arise. The prepare-two-contrasting-monologues-of-up-to-two-minutes-duration-each type of audition, although it may be appropriate for professional organizations, is a very unsatisfactory method of conducting amateur auditions.

In some organizations, a combination prepared and cold reading is used. The auditioner first presents her prepared audition piece, then reads a prepared or unprepared scene from the script, usually with the stage manager or another auditioning actor. (The director may read with an actor on rare occasions, but usually only because no other person is available.) This method gives the director an op-portunity to see the actor at least twice. Unless the actor reads from the script with other auditioners, however, the director cannot very well determine her ability to interact with others in the scene, nor does it allow the director to mix and match the actors to determine the best casting combination.

The most prevalent method of conducting auditions in an ama-teur organization is for the actors to read short sections of a couple of different scenes from the script, usually in pairs. Unless the talent pool is very large, this will allow every auditioner several opportuni-ties to read for the director. Each auditioner will read for a variety of roles, as appropriate, and with a variety of partners, to give the di-rector ample opportunity to assess each actor's abilities. The empha-sis is on the interactive aspects of the audition and on trying to dis-cern the actor's true talent and potential within the context of this particular play.

Begin a typical audition with a few words of welcome and make any necessary introductions—yourself, the stage manager, the pro-ducer, anyone else at the director's table. It's important to maintain a relaxed but professional attitude throughout. Put the auditioners at ease—tell them you know how difficult it is for them to do their best when they have only a few short minutes on stage, that you will give everyone an ample opportunity to be heard, that you know that they will do well, and wish them luck . . . er . . . tell them to break a leg.

Then do a first reading of two to four minutes each in which the actors present a prepared monologue or do a cold reading from the script. Try to assess the actors' overall talent and ability in relation to the criteria that you have established for the roles. After everyone has had an opportunity to read a scene or present a monologue, proceed to a second round (another two to four minutes each) of readings from the script. If time allows, give some limited direction to the actors to asses their ability to take direction and their ability to use that direction imaginatively and skillfully.

Avoid "auditions by the numbers," in which each auditioner is given a number to pin to her clothing. It's not more efficient or more fair or more professional. It's demeaning. Every auditioner deserves to be treated as an person, not as a number. Use each auditioner's name whenever you address her or him. It helps personalize a sometimes impersonal process.

Under no circumstances should you embarrass or ridicule an auditioner. No snickering, and no rude or untoward remarks. It takes a great deal of courage to get up there and put one's whole self on the line for something as nonessential to life as a role in a play. Respect the auditioner's courage, if nothing else, and keep your remarks to yourself.

The Rotation Method ■ One time-effective way to give each actor at least two readings, possibly more, is the rotation method. Begin with a two-person scene—a scene from *Romeo and Juliet,* for example. Choose a Romeo and a Juliet to read the scene. After the first reading, retain the Juliet, but substitute another actor as Romeo. Have the second Romeo read with the first Juliet, then change the Juliet. The second Romeo reads again, this time with the second Juliet, and so on through all the prospective Romeos and Juliets. (Be sure to give the first Romeo—the one who read only once—one more chance to read before you change the scene.) After the first scene has been read, change the scene (or vary the scene as you go along) and repeat the process with another set of actors. This method works equally well for same-sex scenes—Juliet and the Nurse, for instance, or Romeo and Benvolio—in which the traditional approach is to have the actors switch parts.

The advantages of the rotation method are:

1. Each actor reads at least twice.
2. Each actor reads with at least two different partners.
3. Each actor may read more than one scene, and for more than one part.
4. The director and stage manager don't need to shuffle résumés and scripts, trying to decide which scene to read, which actors to read them, and which actors have already read once (or twice or three times).

This is not brain surgery or rocket science. It's a matter of basic organization balanced with respect and consideration for the talents of the individual auditioners.

Callbacks ■ Survivors of the first set of auditions proceed to callbacks. At the first callback, use two-person scenes from the play. Impose some basic direction on the actors as they read. Watch how they respond to your direction and how they relate to one another, as actors *and* as people. Get on stage with the actors if you can. Try to get some sense of what it would be like to work with them, as a director *and* as an actor. Look for the light in their eyes that tells you that somebody's home—a living, breathing, and thinking person.

Ask your actors questions—about themselves, about the scene, about the play—and *listen* to their answers. Listen to the words they use, and how they use them. Listen for intelligence, awareness, understanding, and imagination.

Mix and match the actors in a scene and start to explore casting combinations. With luck, you could have the show cast before the callbacks are over. If you don't, have a second callback to resolve any remaining choices. Follow the same general plan as before but impose more direction on the actors in the scene.

Occasionally, actors may fail to return for callbacks. If they do so without notice or explanation, eliminate them from consideration. If an actor notifies you that she is unable to attend callbacks for some legitimate reason, you can schedule a separate callback if you feel you need to. If the role is minor, you probably won't need to. If, however, the actor is being considered for a major role and you feel you would not be able to cast the play without seeing this person audition further, arrange a mutually acceptable time and place to hold a separate callback. To avoid the appearance of favoritism, invite others who you are considering for major roles to come as well. It's better not to hold a special callback or audition for only one person. First, you will not be able to get a good sense of the chemistry between and among the leading contenders for the major roles.

Second, word of a special callback to which no other actor is invited will likely cause hard feelings among the other auditioners.

It doesn't take very long for an experienced director to decide for or against casting an actor. It can be done in less than a minute in most cases. What takes so long is making sure that each actor feels she had a fair hearing, a fair chance for the role, and that you have had an opportunity to assess fully each actor's abilities and talents.

In auditions, be patient, be polite, but be firm. Give everyone a reasonable chance to be heard and to do their best. You owe the actors this much, even those you have no intention of casting. After that, it's a judgment call. If you've heard everyone read and a have a good sense of how you will cast them, how you manage the rest of the audition is up to you.

If there is time remaining, try out the various combinations of the actors whom you will likely cast. You may eliminate the need for a callback. Occasionally you may discover talent you somehow overlooked in the initial readings. At worst, the actors you intend to cast will become increasingly familiar with the script.

If time is short, or if you have accomplished all that you intended to accomplish, call a halt. Thank everyone for coming and tell them when and where the callback list or cast list will be posted (or when they can expect to be telephoned by the stage manager). If you have planned ahead (as any good director should), you will have scheduled the auditions to end before you think they actually will. Then when the auditions run overtime (as they invariably do), you will have a good reason to wrap things up. Apologize for having to run late in order to give everyone a fair chance to be heard, thank everyone for attending, gather up your notes, and leave. Now is not the time to visit with the actors. You have work to do. Let your stage manager collect the scripts and field the postaudition questions.

CHOOSING THE CAST

Your casting will be determined by the demands of the script and by your preaudition criteria, of course, but may be influenced by other personal and organizational considerations as well. There is the idea of "looking to the future," for instance—giving emerging talent an opportunity to perform. A director might also purposely cast new faces, to enliven the standard mix of actors who are usually cast. In a training situation, the director needs to consider the educational goals of the institution and the educational value of being cast in the production to the individual actor. One student actor may walk through a role easily; another may learn a great deal from being cast in a role just slightly out of her reach.

Casting decisions must be balanced by clearly defined personal, organizational, and script-oriented priorities. Oddly enough, most of your casting choices will fall neatly into place if you follow some general guidelines.

First, be conservative, particularly if you are inexperienced. Your first few directing efforts will be difficult enough without "creative casting." Stick very closely to your preaudition criteria. As you acquire more experience and an improved intuitive casting sense, you can experiment a little more and take more calculated casting risks.

Young or Old? ■ Cast as close to age as possible. If an actor of the right age is not available, cast a younger person to play an older role rather than an older person to play a younger one. An audience will accept a young actor playing an older role far more readily than they will accept an older actor playing a younger role.

Talent or Type? ■ Whom do you choose—the actor who is the perfect type for the role, or the actor who is not quite right for the part but who is an overall better actor? It is a constantly recurring casting question, and one that rightly deserves attention.

In amateur theatre, the matter of talent versus type is essentially no contest. No matter how much an actor looks the part physically, choose acting talent over type every time and you will never have cause to regret your decision. Rarely will type alone sustain an actor in a role. Talent alone *will* sustain the actor, and, by extension, the production. The typecast actor may well be adequate for the role but will rarely prove exceptional. The talented actor will grow into the role, often surprisingly well, and can sometimes achieve exceptional results.

Educational theatres are in the enviable position of being able to offer roles to actors that avoid typecasting and at the same time expand the individual actor's range and experience. Community theatres are slightly less able to cast solely for talent, because there is usually a more limited acting pool. Unlike educational or community theatres, high-level professional companies can afford to wait (or search) until they find that rare combination of talent *and* type.

Unless your casting is totally off-the-wall, the audience will probably not even notice that you didn't cast for type. Few audience members come to the theatre with preconceptions about casting: they don't know the play that well. Most have never seen the play before; in all likelihood they will simply accept the actor you place before them. Cast for talent. You'll never regret it.

Mix and Match ■ Once you have a good idea of whom you want to cast in your production, mix and match actors and roles until you get the best combination—not necessarily the best actors in every role, but the best *combination* of actors. Remember that a director's first responsibility is to ensure a unified production—all the elements of the production working together toward the common goal of unified artistic expression. Balance the casting for the greatest good of the production.

Mixing and matching opens up interesting possibilities that may not otherwise have occurred to you. When others compliment you on an inspired bit of casting, you needn't tell them that you didn't have anybody else for the role or that all you did was shuffle names around on the kitchen table.

You will probably have difficulty casting at least one role in your production. At times you will have to make some casting compromises. Occasionally, you may find that you are unable to cast a good actor because the cast mix isn't right. You may be tempted to use the good actor anyway, and then cast around her for the rest of the roles. Unless you're casting a star role in a musical, avoid sacrificing the entire production for the sake of one actor. Casting around an actor is invariably detrimental, because the balance will be thrown off. All future decisions will evolve from the initial imbalance.

There will also be at least one role in which you will have to settle for an actor about whose ability to handle the role you have serious doubts or misgivings. Sometimes, casting this person isn't even a choice; she's all you've got. Remember, though, that actors love a challenge, and the challenge of this role may be just what this actor needs to shine. (However, you should never express your misgivings to any actor you cast.)

There may be times when you are engaged to direct a star vehicle. No disgrace there. Understand, however, that the priorities in such a production will be significantly skewed to afford the star the most favorable environment in which to display his or her particular talents or abilities. The balance of power in such a production also shifts dramatically. It may be *you* who is expendable, as well as any other element of the production that does not adequately support the star.

Side by Side ■ Occasionally you will be considering two or three or more actors for the same role, but you can't decide between or among them. Divide and conquer. Place two actors in front of you. Decide which of these two actors you prefer. Consider each actor in relation to the criteria that you determined for the role prior to auditions and in relation to each other. When you've decided in favor of one of these two actors, put your choice next to one of the remaining contenders. Repeat the process. Decide. Repeat as often as necessary to determine the final casting.

Still can't decide? Try this technique: flip a coin—heads for one actor, tails for the other. Toss the coin. Your decision will be made while the coin is in the air. Subconsciously (perhaps even consciously), you already favor one actor over the other, if ever so slightly, and you hope the coin will confirm your choice. You don't even have to look at the coin when it lands. Put it back in your pocket. You've already decided.

Should this method fail (it rarely does), and if it is truly of no consequence which actor is chosen for the role (it rarely is), use whatever arbitrary method you can devise. Toss the résumés in the air and cast the actor whose résumé lands face up. Blindfold yourself and throw darts at headshots on the wall. Pull the names out of a hat. If it comes down to this, though, perhaps there was something you missed in the audition and casting process that you should review. It's much better to have another callback, or take another serious look at your casting criteria, than to let the all-too-fickle fates decide the course of your production.

Directing Yourself ■ It is said that a lawyer who represents himself has a fool for a client. Perhaps there is something to be learned there for directors as well. Few good directors are equally good actors. Few good actors are equally good directors. Certainly there are exceptions, which, as they say, simply prove the rule. If you want to direct, then by all means direct. If you want to act, then find somebody else to direct you. If you want to do an injustice to directing and to acting, then direct yourself. Your directing will suffer, your acting will suffer, and your production will suffer. (If you really want to make theatrical history, direct yourself in a musical.)

CASTING GUIDELINES IN A NUTSHELL

- Determine casting criteria prior to auditions.
- Choose intelligence and imagination.
- Choose more experienced over less experienced.
- Choose talent over type.
- Choose real age over age makeup.
- Choose younger to play older, rather than older to play younger.
- Choose inherent stage personality—presence—over technical ability.
- Choose easily directed over resistant or reluctant.
- Choose good attitude and positive, upbeat personality.

- Choose availability for rehearsals, minimal rehearsal conflicts.
- Mix and match for the best possible combination of actor and roles.

Throughout the rehearsal process you will be appealing to the actors you cast through their imaginations, emotions, and intelligence. Make sure the actors you cast possess these qualities in reasonable if not abundant supply.

POSTING THE CAST LIST

Let the stage manager do it. It's her job. Make sure she includes a short note thanking all who auditioned and conveying any information the cast needs to know regarding upcoming rehearsals, where to pick up their scripts and rehearsal schedules, and so on.

Ask those who are cast to initial their name on the cast list, indicating, first, that they accept the role and, second, that they have seen the cast list and have read the information it contains. If you're missing some initials after a day or two (certainly before the first rehearsal, and particularly if scripts and schedules have not been picked up), have your stage manager follow up to find out if there is a problem. (Sometimes actors are so excited they forget to initial the cast list or to read the other information.)

If the tradition in your theatre is to telephone those who are cast (and sometimes those who are not), let the stage manager do that too, at least those who were *not* cast. It's less personal, but it's also less likely to be confrontational. If you have to do it yourself, keep your conversations short, particularly if you are delivering bad news. Don't get caught up in a lengthy discussion about the casting. Express your regrets, thank them for auditioning, invite them to audition again in the future, and get off the phone before they have time to ask uncomfortable or disconcerting questions.

Always be prepared to cast another actor if for any reason an actor is unable or unwilling to accept the role. If it's necessary to hold additional auditions, do so. Better to take the time to make a well-informed choice than to make a hurried or impulsive decision. It may or may not be necessary to delay rehearsals to accomplish additional auditions or callbacks. If possible, begin rehearsals as scheduled. You may have to shift the blocking schedule around to allow for the missing actor, but at least you'll be underway and gathering momentum.

POSTAUDITION STRESS SYNDROME—YOURS AND THEIRS

Sometimes there is no getting around it. One or more actors are going to come up to you or phone you after the cast list is posted and ask you why they weren't cast in the show, why they didn't get such-and-such a part, or what you thought of their audition. Most will be legitimately concerned and interested in learning from the audition process. A few just want to confront you or let off steam.

Some directors refuse to discuss auditions. Most, however, will make at least a reasonable effort to discuss an audition as honestly and objectively as the questioner will allow. Don't discuss the actual casting or your personal casting process. Make no actor-to-actor comparisons. Discuss only the strengths and/or weakness of this particular actor. Never argue with an actor over casting. Explain that casting is often a very subjective process and that there is no adequate way to explain the final casting for a show. Mention that good actors are sometimes not cast simply because there is no appropriate role for them.

Rehearsal Time Lines and Design Meetings 3

*T*he production period is a time for merging and blending the diverse artistic and technical aspects of a production, growing together as individuals with many different and divergent skills and personalities, and gradually realizing a common goal—the performance. The overall responsibility for organizing and managing the production process is the director's.

Some directors are highly organized. They know exactly what's going to happen from one day to the next (sometimes hour by hour and minute by minute) and adhere very closely (religiously, compulsively, pathologically) to their production schedule. Other directors are much less structured and prefer to work more spontaneously. If you are one of the latter, be sure you have a very competent stage manager who can keep you on track throughout the production period.

Naturally, your rehearsal schedule will reflect your method of working. A rehearsal schedule should be organized and detailed enough to allow thorough preparation but flexible enough to accommodate changes, revisions, or inspirations along the way. Keep in mind that no matter what your method of directing, there are certain things that must happen by certain times, and specific tasks that must be accomplished over the course of the rehearsal period if the show is to open on time and in good order.

Types of Rehearsals

There are a number of different types of rehearsals, each with its own objectives and practical considerations.

READ-THROUGH REHEARSAL

From the very beginning of the rehearsal process, every actor should feel that he or she is a vital and integral part of the production. Therefore the entire acting company should be called for this rehearsal, even if some cast members have no lines.

Invite the designers and the head of each department to attend as well, and the producer or a representative of the front office. Including the designers and other members of the production staff in this rehearsal imparts a sense of the whole production, the combined endeavor—everyone working together, onstage and backstage. Ask the set and costume designers to prepare a short presentation (five minutes, more or less) for the cast, and ask the head of each department to be prepared to say a few words about each of their specialties.

Do not immediately distribute the scripts at the beginning of the rehearsal. If you do, no one in the cast will pay any attention to anything that you or anyone else says, because they'll be thumbing through the scripts looking for their parts. If the scripts have been distributed to the cast previously, ask that they be put aside until they're needed.

If you are not making many cuts or changes to the script, let the actors pick up their copy of the script as soon as possible after the cast list is posted. This way, they can begin to familiarize themselves with the script before rehearsals begin. Minor cuts can be marked quickly and efficiently during the first read-through. If, however, you do considerable cutting or revising, it is best to indicate the cuts and changes—you should retype and recopy the script if it's much revised—before the scripts are distributed. This way, you avoid a lengthy cutting process at the read-through and you avoid the inevitable disappointment that actors will feel at losing some (any) of their lines.

The read-through is an opportunity for the cast to meet one another, the designers and heads of backstage departments, the stage manager, and you. The cast should also be introduced to your concept for the play, be given some idea of the set and costumes for the show, and be advised of rehearsal procedures and overall expectations. Not much will actually be accomplished regarding the script, other than a basic familiarity with the flow of words and action. You shouldn't really expect much more than this of the first read-through. Just getting everyone familiar with the script and one another and oriented for the start of the production process is objective enough.

Begin by welcoming everyone and making general announcements. Introduce the producer or the producer's representative and let him say a few words as well. Next, talk about your intended approach to the play, the period, the style, and so on. Introduce the designer(s) and the head of each department and let each make a brief presentation. The members of the cast may never see some of these people again, yet it is important for them to be aware of their contributions to the production. Thank the production staff for attending, and see them out as the stage manager distributes the scripts or asks the cast to get ready to use them.

Introduce the stage manager last and let him talk about his manner of working and his expectations regarding rehearsal behavior (if appropriate to the experience level of the cast).

If minor roles are as yet unassigned, you may assign them now or wait until blocking rehearsals, when you will have a better idea of who is available for the bit parts and walk-ons. If you decide to wait, have the stage manager or an assistant read any unassigned roles. Make any necessary cuts or last-minute changes to the script. Explain to the actors that they must become intimately familiar with the script, above and beyond any and all other tasks that lie before them. Once you are ready to begin the reading, ask the actors to read for context, for meaning, and for a general familiarity with the flow of words and action, but to avoid acting. Then let them proceed.

Don't interrupt the read-through to explain the text, to make comments about the set or lighting or special effects, to compliment individual actors on their reading, or to engage in a lengthy question-and-answer session with the actors regarding the interpretation of the play. Some directors correct mispronunciations as they occur during the reading. Others prefer to note mispronounced words in their script for later reference. Take a short "intermission" at the appropriate point(s) in the script, but otherwise let the reading proceed without interruptions.

When the read-through is completed, make a few generally encouraging remarks about the play and the cast, and let the stage manager remind cast members of their upcoming rehearsals, costume calls, publicity photos, and similar important matters. Be enthusiastic, and give the impression of looking forward with great anticipation to the rehearsal process. Then let everyone go home.

Some directors like to proceed straight to rehearsals, by scheduling a same-day rehearsal following the read-through—the read-through in the morning or afternoon, a break for lunch or dinner, followed by an afternoon or evening rehearsal. This is often done in summer stock, or when the rehearsal period is particularly short. Other directors prefer to come back for the beginning of blocking rehearsals on another day. Much depends on the director's own preference, how long the read-through takes, and the length of the rehearsal period. If a same-day rehearsal is scheduled, be sure to tell the cast well in advance.

You may choose to schedule more than one sit-down read-through. The objectives for any subsequent read-through(s) are relatively the same as for the first—familiarity with the script, with you, and with one another. There is something oddly satisfying, even comforting, about a leisurely read-through of the script—two, three, even four times. Yes, you know your cast can read, but they're learning the play and getting to know one another. There comes a time, however, when you need to get the actors off their backsides and on their feet. Schedule enough read-throughs and you'll discover exactly the point at which you need to do that—when the actors can no longer stay in their seats as they read through the play. It's time to move on.

Blocking Rehearsals—Getting the Show on Its Feet

Divide each rehearsal period into reasonable and manageable blocks of time, and call only those actors you need to accomplish the intended objectives for that particular time period. There is no need, at any time during the rehearsal process (other than the read-through) to call the entire company of actors if the entire company is not needed. There is nothing more mind-numbing and demeaning to an actor than to sit through two hours of rehearsal, walk onstage for two or three lines, then sit down again for another hour or so, only to be told he is no longer needed and sent home.

Begin and end your rehearsals *on time.* If you break the rehearsal down into manageable sections (which you should), respect those time commitments. Don't keep actors waiting arbitrarily or unnecessarily. Respect the time of those with whom you work as you would expect them to respect yours. Apologize for any inconvenience to an actor, and any unforeseen imposition on his time, even when it's not your fault.

There are as many approaches to blocking a show as there are directors, but the blocking process usually resembles one of these three: (1) inspirational/intuitive blocking; (2) "saltshaker" blocking, and (3) the combination technique. To some extent, the inspirational/intuitive method is a part of every blocking rehearsal, although some directors rely on it almost exclusively. The danger in relying on this method to the exclusion of all others is that inspiration and intuition sometimes fail, most notably when the director is under deadline pressure or working with an inexperienced cast.

The saltshaker method—also known as the pushpin-on-the-ground-plan method or the toy-soldiers-on-the-miniature-set method—requires that much of the blocking be decided in advance. This method, too, has its limitations. A rigid adherence to preplanned blocking patterns fails to make allowance for the welcome inspirations of the moment—those happy accidents that arise in the course of every creative endeavor.

The combination technique provides a balance between the two and can be tailored to the experience, abilities, and desires of the director and the talent and experience of the cast. One director may tend toward the intuitive method and another toward the saltshaker method, but each method is balanced to some extent by the other, thereby giving the director the greatest possible creative range within the limitations of the production.

In some instances, the time available for rehearsals may determine the blocking method used. In summer stock, for example, where four plays and one musical in ten weeks may be the norm, the multiple rehearsals per day (not to mention the evening performance) simply do not allow time for extensive exploration of blocking and stage business. In this case, it may be best for the director to block much (or all) of the play in advance (certainly in advance of each rehearsal), adhere closely to the preplanned blocking in rehearsals, and adjust or improve the stage movement as time permits. This approach is not very inspirational, perhaps not even very creative, but it is efficient.

The size of the cast and the level of experience and ability of the actors will also influence the director's choice of blocking method. A large or inexperienced cast requires a certain amount of imposed and somewhat inflexible blocking, whereas a small, experienced cast may be allowed considerably greater leeway to explore the necessary action of the script and to provide their own observations and inspirations regarding blocking and other stage business. Since no two production situations are ever exactly the same, neither will be the choice, or precise balance, of blocking methods.

Blocking is accomplished most quickly and efficiently if you determine the essential action and movement of a scene in advance; accommodate as much inspiration during rehearsals as time, the actors, and production limitations allow; set the blocking; and move on to the next scene. Give the cast a chance to live with the blocking for a reasonable period of time, then adjust or improve it as necessary, time permitting.

The objective for blocking rehearsals is to establish the overall pattern of movement and the physical relationships of the characters and to start the actors on the path toward developing individual physical characterizations. A blocking rehearsal is not the time to conduct an in-depth psychological analysis of the characters or to debate the social/political/economic implications of the play. There will be time for that later.

MEMORIZATION

In most situations, it is counterproductive to have the cast memorize the entire script before the first blocking rehearsal. Certainly they can be familiar with the script, perhaps even have begun to memorize sections of it. But if the actors memorize the script and you make changes to it during rehearsals, their level of frustration will rise and the level of creativity and cooperation will fall dramatically. You made them waste all that time memorizing something you knew would change!

If, however, time is short (summer stock again comes to mind), and you expect that very few changes will be made to the script, you might advise (or require) your cast to get a head start on memorization: to memorize the first few scenes before rehearsals begin and to stay a few scenes ahead during the balance of the blocking rehearsals.

Encourage your cast to learn the blocking and the lines *at the same time*—to walk through the blocking of a scene while memorizing it—to help reinforce the bond between words and action. This way, the lines and the blocking will become inextricably linked. Each reinforces the other, a powerful aid in memorization, and a valuable prompt during performances. If an actor forgets a line but remembers the blocking, the act of moving will very often trigger the forgotten line, because the lines and the blocking have become interdependent elements of the same experience. This interesting phenomenon helps instill a tremendous sense of security and confidence in the actor. He knows that even if he forgets a line, his predetermined movement will help him remember what to say. Few actors forget their blocking in the same way they occasionally forget their lines, but the method works both ways—the lines also reinforce and prompt the blocking.

ENRICHING REHEARSALS—MAKING IT GOOD

Enriching rehearsals are sometimes known as "working rehearsals," and are usually combined with blocking rehearsals. First you block the scene, or parts of it. Then you run the scene to get some sense of continuity and the overall physical shape. Then you "work" the scene, a little at a time, enriching it as you go along. The actors become familiar with the blocking and movement patterns of their characters, the flow of the scene, and their interaction with the other characters. As the understanding of the character in his environment grows, each actor will be able to add more depth to the character, to give it life and an increased sense of believability, within the framework you have provided.

The objectives of enriching rehearsals are to refine stage movement and physical characterization—the process that was begun in blocking rehearsals—and to start exploring the mental and emotional states of the individual characters in the play. The enriching aspect of rehearsals is the time to begin developing the psychological and emotional state of the characters, *after* the essential action of the play—the blocking, character interaction, and individual character movement—has been well established.

POLISHING REHEARSALS—MAKING IT BETTER

Once the blocking settles in and the scene has been worked to a certain level of physical and intellectual continuity, you can begin polishing the scene. One of the clearest indications that you have moved on to the polishing stage is when your actors start to ask intelligent and probing questions regarding their movement, their characters, their motivations, and other aspects of character development and character interaction. The actors will integrate your responses to their questions into their work, and the characters in the play will begin to take on a life of their own.

Listen for the words your actors use when referring to their characters. You will be able to discern a great deal about where the actor is in the development process by the questions he asks and the statements he makes about his character. Semantic changes reflect a noticeable shift in the actor's attitude toward his character—He *would do this-and-such,* or I *[as the character] would do this,* instead of, *My* character *would do this.* The characters become increasingly more personalized, significantly more real, and much less abstract.

The objectives are to refine the stage movement (thereby forwarding the plot), to build the characters, and to clarify the theme of the play. The theme is revealed only through movement—through the physical action of the play (one character speaking to another is a physical action just like any other). Something has to happen, physically, to convey the theme of the play to the audience. (Program notes alone won't help clarify the theme if it doesn't also happen on stage.)

FIX-IT REHEARSALS—MAKING IT BEST

In contrast to a run-through (see below), in which a scene or act (or the entire play) is run without stopping, a fix-it, or run-fix, is a stop-and-go rehearsal. To understand a play completely, to build the best possible production that you can, you need to take it all apart, one piece at a time, refine and polish that piece, and then put it all back together, bit by precious bit. You begin with a predetermined section of the play, and you progress through that part, sometimes only one line at a time, fixing things (and further enriching them) as you go along.

Explain to the cast the absolute necessity for this kind of rehearsal. Solicit their patience, understanding, and support. More often than not, they will follow you to the ends of the earth, as long as they understand the necessity of what you are doing and they can see the long-term advantages to themselves and to the production.

Actors want everything they do on stage to be the best it can be, and they rely on you to help them accomplish that goal. It's perfectly acceptable to be demanding of your actors. In fact, it's your duty and your responsibility. Don't accept less than an actor's full commitment to the role and to the production. Actors will not resent reasonable demands you place on them, but will welcome the challenge and do their absolute best. Actors want to please you, the director, as much as they want to please an audience. They want to prove to you that they were the best choice for the role and that you were right to choose them out of everybody else who auditioned. They want to meet or exceed your expectations. It's up to you to give them every opportunity to do so.

There is only a limited amount of time in which to accomplish a limited amount of fixing, so you will have to pace yourself. You cannot afford to spend a great deal of time polishing the early scenes at the expense of later scenes. We've all been associated with productions in which the first act was extremely well prepared and the second act was a rough framework of barely remembered lines and tentative blocking. This is the result of poor planning on the part of the director. Fix what you can within the available time frame. Sometimes, things must simply go unfixed. It can't be helped. It's the nature of the work.

RUN-THROUGHS—MAKING IT FLOW

Continuity is the key in run-throughs. Actors need to develop a clear sense of where their character is coming from, and where their character is going—physically, mentally, and emotionally—in relation to other characters and in relation to the play as a whole.

It's important that you don't interrupt a run-through unnecessarily. Stay in your seat, sit still, shut up, and pay attention. There is no need for you jump up and "save" the scene. Note any problems, and let the actors press on until the scene is finished (or until it self-destructs). If you constantly interrupt, you destroy the whole point of the rehearsal, that of giving some sense of continuity to the scene and of imparting to the actors some sense of the natural progression of cause and effect that lies at the heart of any play. If you repeatedly interrupt the flow of the rehearsal, the actors will eventually give up, disheartened. They'll recite their lines and walk through their parts without any commitment to the scene, because they know you'll be popping up on stage at any second to fix something.

If it *is* necessary for you to interrupt the rehearsal to make changes, when you once again resume the scene, pick up the action at some point prior to where you interrupted the scene. This will give the actors an opportunity to get back into the scene, to regain their concentration and commitment to the scene, and to integrate the changes more completely into the overall flow of action.

There are three major goals of run-throughs: (1) physical continuity; (2) intellectual continuity, and (3) emotional continuity. A secondary objective is to assess the effectiveness of the production in revealing action, character, and theme. Major restructuring of any element of the production would be ill advised at this point in the rehearsal process. Certainly, minor adjustments can be made to achieve a better balance of plot, character, and theme, but massive reconstruction of the basic framework would only undermine the effectiveness of the entire production (not to mention the toll it would take on the mental and emotional state of the cast and crew). The time to fix the play is past. It is now time to prepare to perform it.

LINE REHEARSALS

Line rehearsals are a courtesy to the actors. It's part of their job to learn the lines, and you should trust them to do it. If you do choose to use line rehearsals, schedule them a day or two before off-book rehearsals.

Inexperienced actors will sometimes ask you if there is a trick or a shortcut to learning lines. Throughout the history of the theatre, from the Ancient Greeks to the present, no one has managed to improve on rote. Every actor from Thespis to Olivier has learned one line at a time. For some it's a long and mostly unexciting process, but it's effective.

Actors should not be left on their own in a line rehearsal. The stage manager should be in charge, and the rehearsal should be conducted as any other, with clearly defined objectives and time limits. Remind the actors that the line rehearsal is not an opportunity for them to *learn* the lines, but to refresh the lines in their minds and imprint them on their memories.

In general, try to dissuade actors from rehearsing scenes together without the presence of the director, the assistant director, or the stage manager. Often, one of the actors will assume the role of director, and start giving notes (usually unwelcome) to the other actors. This can engender hard feelings between and among the actors. Occasionally running lines is fine. Rehearsing scenes is not.

INDIVIDUAL REHEARSALS

The director schedules individual rehearsals to work with one or two actors on individual problems. There is no way to anticipate whether individual coaching or scene work will be necessary. Schedule individual rehearsals as needed, and put a note to that effect in the rehearsal schedule.

SPECIAL REHEARSALS

These may include rehearsals for any out-of-the-ordinary stage business: fight choreography, love scenes, death scenes, nude scenes, and the like. Special rehearsals should be held well before the special activity is to be included in regular rehearsals. A fight scene scheduled to be included in a rehearsal on Thursday should not be choreographed the day before. Let the relative complexity of the activity be your guide, and plan accordingly.

There are a number of plays (and a musical or two) in which there are nude (or nearly nude) scenes or in which, in the opinion of the director, a scene could be played nude. Certainly nude scenes can be cut or done clothed, but the integrity of the play may be compromised—to a greater or lesser extent, depending on the relative importance of the scene to the play. If nudity is a consideration in the initial choice of the play, it's better to choose a play without nudity than to cut or diminish the scene and thereby do an injustice to the play and to the playwright. Nudity in a scene will attract a great deal of attention and interest, however, generally out of proportion to the scene's importance. At the very least, nudity onstage is distracting to the audience. In some cases, it can completely disrupt or even destroy the flow of the play.

A nude scene should be approached with great care. To integrate the scene into the play, you must lay the groundwork well in advance. Characterization and character interaction are the key. The audience must accept that this character would do that and that these characters would interact that way in that situation, as a natural extension of the characters' personalities. In other words, the audience has to see it coming. They must be mentally and emotionally prepared for the scene, so that when it does occur, the distraction (or shock) will be minimal, and they can be drawn back into the scene very quickly.

If you do a play with a nude scene, mention it at the auditions and in all preaudition announcements. Under no circumstances should you spring it on the cast midway through the rehearsal period. Be honest and straightforward about the scene from the beginning.

There is no need for the actors to appear nude at auditions. Reserve the clothing optional audition for callbacks, if at all. A bathing suit audition is often sufficient, even then. A bathing suit doesn't reveal everything, but modern bathing suits leave very little to the imagination, and you can ask about anything else: tattoos, for instance, or other physical peculiarities.

Hold minimal-clothing auditions privately, away from prying eyes. Keep the audition staff to a minimum—the director, assistant director, stage manager, and (oddly enough, considering the context) the costumer should be plenty. The audition staff should include both males and females. Also be certain that no actor is physically touched in any way by any member of the staff during the auditions, and that the audition is conducted in an aboveboard, matter-of-fact, and professional manner.

Once you have decided on your tentative cast and *before* you've posted the cast list, discuss the nude scene with your potential choices. As best you can, try to determine their real feelings. Appearing nude onstage may seem perfectly acceptable to some actors *in the abstract* (and when it's somebody else), but the reality may be entirely different. They may have agreed to do the scene in order to be cast, thinking they'd be able to get out of it later. Or they may have fully intended to do the scene but find themselves increasingly inhibited as the performance date approaches.

There is no compelling need for the actors to rehearse in the nude until production week, unless they choose to do so. Rehearsing nude, or nearly so, in front of their peers will be more difficult for some than appearing nude before an audience. The audience is distant, and, for the most part, impersonal. Fellow cast members are not. If the actors can perform the scene in rehearsal without serious inhibitions, performing nude in front of an audience should not be a problem. Suggest that the actors think of nudity as a costume like any other, and remind them that it is the characters who are appearing nude, not they. It may help ease the tension.

You may wish to prepare the nude scene separately from the rest of the play, during special rehearsals. Ask the actors how *they* prefer to approach the scene. Some may wish to tear off their clothes and jump right in. Others may choose to sneak up on it, by gradually becoming accustomed to greater stages of undress as rehearsals progress. Let the actors choose the method, but defer to the most conservative approach if there is a difference of opinion. Whatever method you choose, don't make it a big deal. Expect and maintain a professional and adult attitude toward the scene, and approach it as you would any other—objectively, sensitively, and honestly.

Never touch or otherwise behave inappropriately toward an unclothed or a partially clothed actor, no matter how well you may know them personally or professionally. You may lose your job, and the odds are that you may never be hired again, certainly not by *this* organization. Likewise, never hold rehearsals with unclothed or partially clothed actors at which you are the only other person present. Always have another member of the production staff in attendance— the stage manager or assistant stage manager, an assistant director—preferably someone of the sex opposite to yours. Keep yourself absolutely clear of potentially compromising situations.

TECHNICAL REHEARSALS

If the objective of enriching rehearsals is to make it good, polishing rehearsals to make it better, fix-it rehearsals to make it best, and run-throughs to make it flow, the objective of technical rehearsals is often simply to make it through.

In some organizations, technical rehearsals are invariably a disaster for everyone involved. This need not be so. Many of the common problems associated with technical rehearsals can be anticipated and accommodated well in advance. If you have prepared the cast and crew for most eventualities, you can then approach the technical rehearsal with minor apprehension (or at least without abject fear).

Very early in rehearsals, for instance, have the stage manager designate on the rehearsal floor (usually with tape) the actual size and placement of the major scenic elements, particularly walls and doors. If there is to be a rug on the floor (always a slippery proposition), import a rehearsal rug and attach it firmly to the floor so the actors can get used to walking on it. Get your stage manager to locate representative pieces of furniture and rehearsal props that approximate the real props in size and weight. If period costumes are to be worn in the show, ask your costume designer to supply rehearsal skirts and shoes (for men as well as women) appropriate to the type and style of costumes the cast will wear in performance. These relatively simple steps can help alleviate the problems that generally arise when the cast works with the set, furniture, costumes, and/or props for the first time. If the cast is secure in their onstage environment, you can concentrate your efforts on the technical areas of the production.

If you have planned ahead (as any good director should), you will have already held "tech only" rehearsals, at which the lighting and/or sound for the show will have been worked out and the backstage crew will have had a chance to practice set changes. You will also have had a "tech watch"—an opportunity for the technical staff to watch a run-through of the show so they can become familiar with the onstage action.

Before the technical rehearsal begins, tell the actors what to expect. Enlist their support, and encourage them to consider the rehearsal a challenge, not an ordeal. This is a perfect opportunity for each of them to test their acting skills by "acting" as if nothing had gone wrong (if, in fact, anything does go wrong), and to prepare themselves for the possibility that something may go wrong in performance. Remind the cast that technical problems are not their concern. They are to persevere, no matter what, unless they feel that their personal safety is at risk.

As the rehearsal progresses, try to remember that nothing is so seriously wrong that it cannot be remedied in time. Right now, *during* the rehearsal, is not the time to try to fix it. You will waste more time than most problems are worth if you interrupt the continuity of the rehearsal in order to effect immediate changes or repairs. Simply make a note of any problems that arise, and press on. Interrupt the rehearsal only for technical problems that stop the show cold or that endanger the physical well-being of the actors or crew.

One other note: from the start of technical rehearsals, encourage the cast to "walk" the stage before the start of each rehearsal and before the house is opened to the audience at each performance. There may be changes or alterations to the set, additional furniture or set dressing, or a slight repositioning of scenic elements—like escape stairs, for instance—that they should be aware of *before* they walk onstage to perform. The stage manager should tell the cast about any changes in the set, of course, but there's no substitute for actually "walking" the stage. No surprise is the best surprise.

The goal of technical rehearsals is to refine the technical elements of the play and to ensure that these technical elements support and enhance the plot, characters, and theme. Major changes to any of the design or technical elements are unwarranted at this point.

Technical continuity is as important as the continuity of any other aspect of the play.

There will be times when things don't come together technically. Something isn't working. In these instances it is often better to do without the offending element rather than try to change it, fix it, or otherwise remanufacture it. Realize, too, that any remanufactured elements will still have to be retested and rehearsed.

Encourage your technical director to have backup systems in place for any mechanical or electrical effect that might fail to perform as advertised. Be prepared at any time to substitute people power for horsepower and to rely on basic, human ingenuity and resourcefulness when the universal laws of mechanics and electricity suddenly, and for no apparent reason, no longer function.

Remember your fallback position—all it takes to make theatre are two planks and a passion, and the planks are optional. You don't need fancy technical effects to make theatre happen. It's nice to have them, of course, to enhance the production, but the bottom line is that you don't really need them. No technical or design element of the play is more important than the play.

COSTUME PARADE

At the costume parade, all the costumes in the production are "paraded," one at a time or in appropriate groupings, in front of the costume designer, set designer, lighting designer, and director. This gives the director and designers an opportunity to see the costumes under the stage lights and against the set. In most instances, the costumes will not be quite finished, nor will the set or lighting be fully completed. No matter. The designers and director simply want to see how the costumes appear in the approximate context of the lighting and setting for the show. That way any necessary adjustments to the lighting, sets, or costumes can be made before technical and dress rehearsals.

A costume parade is generally scheduled a week or so before the technical or dress rehearsal at which finished costumes are expected. The costume parade may be separate from or part of a regularly scheduled rehearsal, depending on the number of costumes, the complexity of the set and lighting, and other relevant factors.

DRESS REHEARSALS—MAKING IT SING

This is the time to bring the production to life. Dress rehearsals should be conducted as near to performance conditions as possible. The actors and crews should have the same "call" as they will for a performance, and the show should start at the regularly scheduled time. There should be no stops during the rehearsal other than for intermissions, except for a "clear and present danger" to the life or limb of cast and crew.

There should be two dress rehearsals, minimum. The actors and crew need to make a smooth transition from rehearsal conditions to performance conditions. Only minor changes to the show should be made after the first dress rehearsal. *No* changes are to be made after the second dress rehearsal. No matter what shape the show is in by the end of the second dress rehearsal, leave it alone. It's too late. Live with it. You can schedule a brushup rehearsal (see page 72) the following week to make these adjustments.

Essentially, a dress rehearsal is a performance without an audience. It gives the cast and crew an opportunity to run the show under performance conditions, without the added concern (or distraction) of an audience. Therefore, the objectives of a dress rehearsal should be to ensure and sustain formal performance conditions and to allow the cast and crew to learn to absorb any problems or difficulties as if they had occurred within the context of an actual performance.

Opening Night

By opening night, your work is nearly done. If you have done your job well, there is every reason to be proud of your work. Even if you have fallen short of your expectations, there is no reason for despair. You did your best, as did everyone else associated with the production. There were many new experiences, much new understanding, and many lessons learned.

Everybody expects *a greenroom speech.* And they expect it to be wise, witty, inspirational, motivational, and nothing short of spectacular. Certainly you can strive to meet these expectations. Realize, however, that anything you say will have no effect whatever on the show. You cannot save a poor production with a rousing greenroom speech. Not the blocking, nor the lighting, nor any other aspect of the production will change because of anything you say. The only thing that you can hope to influence—positively, upliftingly—is the emotional and mental state of the performers.

Keep your speech short, upbeat, and simple. No matter how difficult the rehearsal process may have been, no matter how small the audience may be, no matter the weather, no matter what, say only positive things. It's still your job to encourage the cast to do the best they possibly can.

If you are at a loss what to say when you're confronted with all those expectant, half-madeup faces, try something like this:

> Is everybody here? Great. Okay, this is it. You've got a good audience out there. They've heard great things about the show, and I know they won't be disappointed. It's been great working with you. You have all done a *great* job, every one of you, and you've all come a long way. You've worked hard, and I'm very proud of you. Now go out there and knock 'em dead! Break a leg, everybody!!

It's simple, straightforward, positive, reinforcing, and best of all, it's short. You needn't be overly dramatic. Sincerity works best.

Some directors make it a point to speak with every member of the cast before the show goes up. If you are one of these directors, try to make the rounds *before* your greenroom speech. Once in the greenroom, you need to say your piece and then leave, so that the actors can use the last few minutes before curtain to prepare for what lies ahead.

Unless you have backstage duties, make yourself scarce during the performance. Make an appearance at intermission to bolster the troops, and stand in the wings after the show to offer your congratulations as the cast comes offstage after the curtain call. Otherwise, don't hover backstage. Trust the cast and crew to do their best, and get out of their way and let them do it.

BRUSHUP REHEARSALS

Brushup rehearsals falls into two categories: (1) a midweek adjustment rehearsal, in which you attempt to fix any major problems that arose during the previous week's performances, or (2) a refresher run-through, to make minor changes to the show (if any) and to get the actors and crew back into the swing of things for the upcoming performances.

An adjustment rehearsal should address only individual problem scenes, or parts of scenes, not the entire play. Fix only what needs to be fixed and leave the rest alone. In contrast, a refresher rehearsal is a full run-through. Minor changes (if any) are noted before the rehearsal; the run-through is not interrupted.

If an adjustment rehearsal is needed, schedule it two days before the performances to follow, and schedule a refresher run-through for the day before performances. If no adjustment rehearsal is needed, simply give the cast the night off.

Adjustment and refresher rehearsals are usually done in street clothes, except when complicated costume changes are part of what needs to be adjusted or refreshed. An adjustment rehearsal uses technical support only as necessary. A refresher run-through is done under performance conditions, with full technical support. Lighting, sound, scene changes, and special effects are executed as in a regular performance. The technicians need to refresh their memories and their timing just as the actors do.

CONTINGENCY REHEARSALS

Contingency rehearsals (which are noted on the rehearsal schedule as TBA) are built-in catch-up days interspersed throughout the rehearsal period, and can serve one of two purposes: (1) a reward, in that the cast can be given a day off if things are going well, if you are ahead of schedule, or if you have just about had it and think everybody might benefit from a day away, or (2) a lifesaver, a show saver and a sanity saver if you are running behind schedule or just barely holding your own.

Use the contingency rehearsal to do whatever needs to be done that you would otherwise have had to steal time away from other rehearsals (or, heaven forbid, schedule additional rehearsals) in order to accomplish.

Once in a while, it helps to shake up the rehearsal regimen, just to break the monotony and allow for a little real-world perspective. Decide, "spontaneously," to suspend a rehearsal, send out for pizza and soda, crank up the sound system with some popular dance tunes (*their* choices, not yours), and let the cast relax, shake it out, recharge, and regroup.

What seems totally spontaneous and off-the-wall should be planned well in advance, of course. Schedule a TBA rehearsal midway through the rehearsal period or after a difficult section of the script. Begin the rehearsal as planned, then at some appropriate point, go into your "spontaneous" act. You need not lose an entire rehearsal for this. An hour-or-so break from rehearsal and then back to work should do the trick.

SUMMARY

Here, in a nutshell, are the major types of preproduction rehearsals and the objectives for each type:

- *Read-Through:*
  Introduce the cast to one another, the designers and heads of departments, the stage manager, and the director.
  Explain the concept for the play and describe the set, costumes, and other technical aspects of the play.
  Orient the cast to the rehearsal process.
  Become familiar with the flow of words and action of the script.

- *Blocking Rehearsals:*
  Establish the basic stage movement patterns and physical character interaction, stage business, and individual physical characterizations.
  Establish the flow of action—the basic physical "plot" of the play.
- *Enriching Rehearsals:*
  Refine stage movement, stage business, character interaction, and individual physical characterization.
  Begin the exploration of the mental and emotional state of the characters and the "world of the play."
- *Polishing Rehearsals:*
  Explore and refine individual characters and character interactions.
  Fine-tune stage movement and stage business.
  Clarify character and reveal the theme in relation to the physical "plot" of the play.
- *Fix-It Rehearsals:*
  Painstakingly disassemble and reassemble each scene to define, explore, and refine its inner workings.
  Discern and reveal the essence of the plot, characters, and theme of the play.
- *Run-Through Rehearsals:*
  Provide continuity—moment to moment, scene by scene, and scene *to* scene.
  Determine the overall effectiveness of the action of the play in revealing plot, characters, and theme.
  Effect any *minor* adjustments in the production to that end.
- *Technical Rehearsals:*
  Refine the technical and design elements of the production in support of the play.
  Ensure that the technical elements of the play enhance the plot, characters, and theme.
- *Dress Rehearsals:*
  Establish the final balance of all the elements of the play under performance conditions.

The Rehearsal Schedule

With some idea of the range of rehearsals at your command and of what is to be accomplished with each type of rehearsal, your next responsibility is to prepare the rehearsal schedule.

There is nothing mysterious or magical about organizing a rehearsal schedule. It is a matter of logistics and logic tempered with experience—a matter of arranging priorities and providing for necessities. Much of what *must* be done will be built into the schedule automatically—opening night, dress rehearsals, technical rehearsals, and so on. Organizing the balance of the schedule is fairly unimaginative. Very clearly defined objectives must be reached by very clearly defined dates and times. How the director gets to these objectives by these dates or times is his primary concern in scheduling. Here are some general notes:

1. You will never have enough time. It won't matter if you have eight, ten, twelve, or fifty-two weeks to rehearse; it still won't be enough. There are just too many things that need to be done. A production, any production, proceeds to a "point of development." No matter where you are in the process, the audience marches into the theatre on opening night expecting a performance. Accomplish what you can within the time allotted. Maximize your gains, cut your losses, and accept the outcome.

2. There is always "a problem." It may be a difficulty with the set or costumes, budget constraints, time constraints, a recalcitrant actor, or one of any number of other challenges. No matter how prepared you are for any eventuality that might conceivably arise during rehearsals, there will always be one thing you have overlooked or could not have possibly foreseen. That one thing will be "the problem," and it will occupy an inordinate amount of your time. You cannot plan for it. The best you can do is accommodate it when it happens and hope you can resolve the problem expediently and with as little negative effect on the production as possible. (Therefore, you schedule one or two contingency rehearsals, just in case.)

3. It is most effective and efficient to work *backward* from opening night. Determine the performance dates first, and fill in your schedule backward toward the start of rehearsals. Decide what you need to accomplish, and in what time frame, and arrange your schedule accordingly, with those goals and objectives as your guides.

4. Feel free to make changes in the rehearsal schedule as the production process demands. No schedule is set in stone. Keep as closely to the schedule as you can, but don't hesitate to change it if you need to. Apologize to the cast and crew for the inconvenience, and make reasonable accommodations for individual problems and conflicts, but remind everyone that it is for the

betterment of the production that you do this inexcusable thing, then move along to the next item of business.

5. If you are working with actors who have lives outside the theatre—in an all-volunteer amateur community theatre, for example—it's better to postpone fine-tuning the rehearsal schedule until after casting, when you've had a chance to talk with your cast and iron out all the conflicts that invariably arise. "Things" always seem to come up, often at the last minute, and you, not they, are expected to adjust. It's a hard fact of amateur theatrical life, but one you must learn to live with. One way to minimize the problem is to provide space on the audition form for the actors to indicate any potential conflicts within the rehearsal and/or performance periods. Remember, though, that auditioners frequently "forget" to mention conflicts because they fear (rightly so) the conflicts may lessen their chances for a role.

WHO'S IN WHAT

The "Who's in What" is a scene-by-scene breakdown of which characters (Who) appear in which scenes (What). A "Who's in What" is especially helpful in a large cast show, a musical (particularly one with a large chorus), or in a show with several nonspeaking roles. Actors often have no idea they are to appear in a scene, as set decoration or a walk-on (or -through), unless they are specifically told (sometimes, unfortunately, after the fact) or unless they have been given a copy of the "Who's in What."

You (or your stage manager) prepare the "Who's in What" character/scene breakdown and distribute it to every member of the cast, nonspeaking roles included. From then on, it's the actor's responsibility to arrive at the appointed time and place for each scene in which he appears. (See the sample "Who's in What" in Appendix A.)

SAMPLE REHEARSAL SCHEDULE

With the general rehearsal guidelines and all the different types of rehearsals in mind, let's plan a fictitious rehearsal schedule.

Assume that the play you're directing is *I Ought to Be in Pictures,* a popular two-act comedy by Neil Simon. There are three characters in the play—two females, Libby and Steffy, and one male, Herb. Act 1 is in two scenes, and is fifty-seven script pages long. Act 2 is in four scenes, and is fifty-one pages long. It's a basic, three-character, modern-dress, one-set, lights-up-lights-down play.

Let's assume further that the show will open on a Friday night, eight weeks from the start of rehearsals, that it will run for two consecutive weekends—Friday through Sunday nights—and that there are no intervening holidays or other special events to consider. Since this is educational or community theatre, there will be no rehearsals on weekends until very near the performance dates. With these limitations, you have a total of approximately forty possible rehearsal days.

Before you can begin mapping out the schedule, you need a copy of the script, a blank ten-week calendar, several sharpened pencils (with good erasers), and—most important—a competent, experienced stage manager. Sit down with your supplies and your stage manager in a quiet place where you won't be disturbed for the next few hours, and begin.

First, mark out eight consecutive weeks on your blank calendar. Number the rehearsal days consecutively, Monday through Friday of each week, from 1 to 40. (See the Sample Rehearsal Schedule in Figure 3–1.)

By the numbers:

1. Indicate *opening night* on Day 40. So far, so good. Now, working backwards . . .
2. Pencil in two *dress rehearsals* on Day 38 and Day 39—Wednesday and Thursday—the two days before opening night.
3. Pencil in a *technical rehearsal* on Day 37—Tuesday—the day before the first dress rehearsal.
4. Pencil in one *run-through* on Day 36—Monday—the day before the technical rehearsal. (This run-through will be run with technical support but is not considered a technical rehearsal.) Since this show is not difficult technically, you've chosen to have one run-through of the show the day before the first technical rehearsal. If this production, or any other production, were more technically complex, you would likely begin the week with a full-blown technical rehearsal, rather than an additional run-through, to give the technicians more time to prepare for performance.
5. Schedule "tech only" rehearsals (also known as "dry techs") on the Saturday and Sunday following Day 35. Also, schedule a "tech watch" for Day 35.
6. Pencil in another *run-through* on Day 35, the Friday before tech-dress week. Add the curtain call to this rehearsal as well.
7. On Day 34, Thursday, pencil in an Act 2 *run-fix*. On Day 33, Wednesday, pencil in an Act 1 *run-fix*. Also schedule a *costume parade* for this rehearsal. You may wish to start the rehearsal a little earlier than usual to accommodate the changing of costumes and the parade. If the costuming for a particular show is

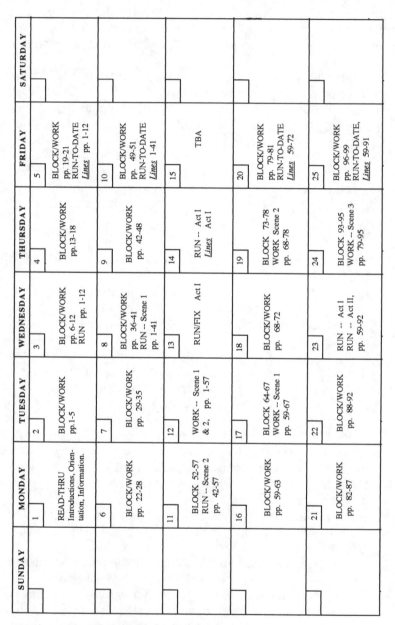

SUNDAY	MONDAY	TUESDAY	WEDNESDAY	THURSDAY	FRIDAY	SATURDAY
	1 READ-THRU Introductions, Orientation, Information.	**2** BLOCK/WORK pp.1-5	**3** BLOCK/WORK pp. 6-12 RUN pp. 1-12	**4** BLOCK/WORK pp.13-18	**5** BLOCK/WORK pp. 19-21 RUN-TO-DATE *Lines* pp. 1-12	
	6 BLOCK/WORK pp. 22-28	**7** BLOCK/WORK pp. 29-35	**8** BLOCK/WORK pp. 36-41 RUN -- Scene 1 pp. 1-41	**9** BLOCK/WORK pp. 42-48	**10** BLOCK/WORK pp. 49-51 RUN-TO-DATE *Lines* 1-41	
	11 BLOCK 52-57 RUN -- Scene 2 pp. 42-57	**12** WORK -- Scene 1 & 2, pp. 1-57	**13** RUN/FIX Act I	**14** RUN -- Act I *Lines* Act I	**15** TBA	
	16 BLOCK/WORK pp. 59-63	**17** BLOCK 64-67 WORK -- Scene 1 pp. 59-67	**18** BLOCK/WORK pp. 68-72	**19** BLOCK 73-78 WORK Scene 2 pp. 68-78	**20** BLOCK/WORK pp. 79-81 RUN-TO-DATE *Lines* 59-72	
	21 BLOCK/WORK pp. 82-87	**22** BLOCK/WORK pp. 88-92	**23** RUN -- Act I RUN -- Act II, pp. 59-92	**24** BLOCK 93-95 WORK -- Scene 3 pp. 79-95	**25** BLOCK/WORK pp. 96-99 RUN-TO-DATE, *Lines* 59-91	

Figure 3-1. Sample Rehearsal Schedule

SUNDAY	MONDAY	TUESDAY	WEDNESDAY	THURSDAY	FRIDAY	SATURDAY
OFF	**26** BLOCK/WORK pp. 100-105	**27** BLOCK/WORK pp. 105-110 RUN -- Scene 4 pp. 96-110	**28** RUN/FIX -- Act II pp.59-110	**29** RUN -- Act II *Lines* -- Act II	**30** TBA	OFF
31 OFF	INDIVIDUAL SCENES, TBA	**32** RUN-THRU Acts I & II	**33** Costume Parade 6PM RUN/FIX Act I	**34** RUN/FIX Act II	**35** RUN-THRU Acts I & II Block Curtain Call ("Tech watch.")	OFF ("Tech only" rehearsal.)
36 OFF ("Tech only" rehearsal.)	RUN-THRU (No costumes, no makeup.) w/Tech support.	**37** TECH REHEARSAL Costume/Makeup Call 7PM Run-Thru 8 PM	**38** DRESS REHEARSAL Call 6 PM Performance 8PM	**39** DRESS REHEARSAL Call 6 PM Performance 8PM	**40 OPENING NIGHT ! !** *Break a Leg !* Call 6PM Performance 8PM	**41** PERFORMANCE Call 6 PM Performance 8PM
42 PERFORMANCE Call 5:30 PM Performance 7:30 PM	**43** OFF	**44** OFF	**45** TBA 7 PM, if scheduled.	**46** RUN-THRU Tech/no costumes. Call 7PM Run-Thru at 8 PM	**47** PERFORMANCE Call 6 PM Performance 8PM	**48** PHOTO CALL 2PM PERFORMANCE Call 6PM Performance 8PM
49 PERFORMANCE Call 5:30 PM Performance 7:30 PM STRIKE Following						

NOTES: -- *Please read carefully* --

1. All rehearsals are from 7 to 10 PM, unless otherwise indicated. Please be on time, and consult your "Whos' in What" for the scenes in which you appear. Also check the Callboard for exact times & characters called for each rehearsal. Contact the Stage Manager immediately regarding any possible conflicts, possible lateness, and so on. Check the Callboard.
2. Individual rehearsals/coaching will be arranged as needed. Check the Callboard.
3. Lines are to be memorized by the dates indicated on the schedule. Please plan ahead. If you need assistance with memorization, please consult with the Stage Manager.
4. You will be advised as far in advance as possible of any changes in the Rehearsal Schedule. Check the Callboard.
5. Check the Callboard **daily** for any notes or changes regarding the Rehearsal Schedule, costume fittings, photo calls, individual rehearsals, and so on. It is your responsibility

extensive or complicated, a separate rehearsal should be scheduled for the costume parade.

8. On Day 32, Tuesday, pencil in a *run-through.*

9. On Day 31, Monday, pencil in *individual scenes,* TBA.

10. Pencil in two rehearsal days as *contingency rehearsals*—one on Day 30 and the other on Day 15. Indicate these rehearsals as TBA. If you have been keeping track (and if you haven't, your very competent stage manager surely has been), you know that you now have twenty-eight rehearsal days left.

11. Pencil in Day 29 as Act 2 *run-through*, and Day 28 as Act 2 *run-fix.* Indicate Day 14 as Act 1 *run-through,* and Day 13 as Act 1 *run-fix.* Running total: twenty-four days left.

12. On Days 25, 20, 10, and 5 pencil in the *second half* of each rehearsal as a *run-to-date* rehearsal. There are two ways to approach a run-to-date rehearsal: (1) as a true run-to-date rehearsal, in which you run *every* scene that has been blocked and worked prior to that rehearsal, or (2) as a "mini" run-to-date rehearsal, in which you run only those scenes that have been blocked and worked since the previous run-to-date rehearsal. It's your choice, but let the cast know what to expect in advance. (On Figure 3–1, both types of run-to-date rehearsals are indicated. The pages—or scenes—to be run are noted below each rehearsal.)

13. To avoid wasting an entire rehearsal period as an *off-book run-through,* indicate on the rehearsal schedule the days by which individual scenes should be memorized. This is usually required for the run-to-date rehearsals, excluding the lines from the one or two rehearsals just prior. Go back through the schedule and pencil in the *off-book* requirements. Write "Lines, pages __ to __," or "Lines, Scene 1," or "Lines, Act 2" on the appropriate date. For this particular play, all of Act 1 should be memorized by Day 14, and all of Act 2 (and, by extension, the entire play) should be memorized by Day 29. Indicate these deadlines on the rehearsal schedule.

14. Finally, move to the beginning of the rehearsal period, and pencil in a *read-through* on Day 1. Indicate on the schedule that the rehearsal will include matters other than simply reading the play—introducing the designers and technical staff, for example. This gives you a basic, bare-bones outline of the rehearsal schedule, containing all essential and necessary rehearsals. The next step is to fill in the rest.

15. You have ten rehearsals to block and work Act 1, and eleven rehearsals to block and work Act 2. This works out to approxi-

mately five or six pages of the script to block and work in each rehearsal. Barring any problems that may arise during the rehearsal period (and assuming that you have done your homework), this is very manageable.

16. The play opens with the characters of Libby and Steffy, and these two characters occupy the stage for the first twelve pages of the script. That very conveniently covers the first two rehearsal periods, Day 2 and Day 3. The third character, Herb, appears for the first time up in the middle of page 12, so he first appears at rehearsals on Day 4.

17. From this point, find appropriate places in the script at which to begin and end rehearsals. On regular days, block and work five or six pages. On days scheduled for a run-to-date rehearsal, do only three pages. Indicate the script page numbers (or scenes) on the rehearsal schedule. Note on the Sample Rehearsal Schedule that a run of pages 1–12 is indicated on Day 3 and that there are other short runs of varying lengths interspersed throughout. Whenever possible, and within the time constraints, *reinforce* what you have done in rehearsal before you go off in another direction, or to another scene. The run is included on Day 3 because the third actor will join the rehearsals the following day, causing a noticeable shift in the direction and focus of rehearsals.

18. On Day 8, run the first scene before starting the second scene the following day. "Runs" can be approached as a run-fix (stop-and-go) rehearsal, or as a true run, without interruptions. The time allotted in the rehearsal for the run will likely allow two complete runs of the material without interruptions (each run preceded or followed by brief notes), or one stop-and-go.

19. Proceed in like manner through the rehearsal schedule.

20. With the process essentially complete, go back though the schedule and fine-tune it. Refer to the script for the most appropriate places to begin and end rehearsals, the actual time allotted to each section of the script, and so on. Schedule line rehearsals, if desired, as well as any other rehearsals you feel would be necessary to prepare the play for performance.

In a separate space on the rehearsal schedule, on the back of it, or on a separate attached page, include any general information regarding the rehearsal schedule that the cast needs to know. (Do it on the same page as the schedule if you can; separate pages can be easily lost or misplaced.) Also include the stage manager's home phone number and the backstage phone number. Be sure these notes are clear and concise. Leave no ambiguities for an actor or crew member to misinterpret or misunderstand. You will not be able to provide for all eventualities, of course, but address as many as you can.

Review the entire schedule for any potential conflicts, discrepancies, typos, or other errors (like incorrect page numbers, for instance), and substitute the actual calendar dates for your rehearsal numbers before you distribute the schedule to the cast and crew.

OTHER CALENDARS AND SCHEDULES

As director, you will be closely involved with the design and technical schedules. You will not, however, *make* the schedules. The technical schedule is the technical director's responsibility, and you would be seriously overstepping the bounds of your authority if you presume to tell him what to do and when to do it. You should be involved with the technical schedule only in an advisory way.

As far in advance of the beginning of rehearsals and as near as to the selection of the play as possible, get together with your stage manager and work out a tentative *master calendar* that encompasses all aspects of production. Then arrange to meet with the designers and the heads of all design and technical departments. Distribute copies of your proposed master schedule, and go through it day by day, item by item, making changes and compromises as necessary.

For the most part, your rehearsal schedule and the technical schedule will not conflict. The technical staff will be working at different hours and in different locations than you and your actors. There are, however, certain, *potential* trouble spots, most likely during the last few week of rehearsals, when all the parts of the production necessarily come together. Most of these potential conflicts involve using the stage. You may schedule an onstage rehearsal when the set is being put up or the lights are being hung and there is no way you can use the space. The best way to avoid such conflicts is to resolve them with the appropriate staff member(s) well in advance.

Here are the major deadlines you should consider in organizing the overall design and technical elements of the master schedule. These are the deadlines that affect you most directly:

- Preliminary set, lighting, sound, and costume designs
- Finished set, lighting, sound, and costume designs
- Rehearsal props
- Final props
- Integration of props, sound into rehearsal (as applicable)
- Costume parade
- No-actor, "technical only" rehearsal(s)

- Technical rehearsals with actors
- Dress rehearsals
- Understudy/replacement rehearsals, when technical support is needed
- Strike

The many other interior technical deadlines are the responsibility of the technical director and the various department heads, not you. You should be aware of them, certainly, but the only reason you will become concerned or involved with them is if a problem arises that directly affects the overall production. Otherwise, you do your job and let the designers and technicians do theirs.

If you expect the sets, lighting, sound, costumes, and special effects all to be done at the same time, you will be seriously disappointed. Schedule different (but reasonable) deadlines for each technical element of the production. This way, any problem in one technical area can be overcome without a major disruption in any other area. Another advantage is that as each deadline is met, the technical personnel working in that area can be shifted into other more pressing areas, thereby increasing the number of people available to work on a more complex or more labor-intensive aspect of the production.

The responsibility for reassigning technical personnel is not yours, of course, but you can facilitate the process by requesting different deadlines for each technical aspect of the production. Ask to have the sound for the show completed by a certain date so you can use it in rehearsal. Ask that the set be completed by a certain date so the actors can get used to the stage space. Once the set is in place, the lights can be hung and focused. And so on. If you ask (or demand) that everything be done on the same day, it's a sure bet that most of what you request will not be ready. Plan ahead.

Preproduction Design Meetings

Theatre is an interpretive art that relies on a close collaboration between and among many artists. Your concept, your vision for the play is the artistic *and* organizational force behind the production. Realizing your personal vision depends, however, to a greater or lesser degree on realizing the visions of all the other artists with whom you are working. It is virtually impossible for any one person—designer, director, or actor—to impose his own interpretation, concept, or vision on the production to the exclusion of all others. It is equally difficult, if not impossible, for any one individual to take full responsibility for every aspect of the production. In other words, you can't do it all no matter how much you sometimes wish you could.

Your responsibility, as I've said, is to ensure the artistic unity of the production. Unity of production is, or should be, the primary goal of every theatre artist, certainly of every theatre artist with whom you work on your production. Any discussions that you have with other artistic personnel should flow from that basic premise, and you should expect that each member of your production team actively supports this goal.

You may find, however, that an agreement on artistic unity in theory does not necessarily indicate an agreement in the *method* of achieving unity, nor does it ensure an artistically unified production. You will be working with people of diverse interests and skills and with sometimes highly divergent personalities. You can expect a certain level of disagreement on how to achieve your common goal. Each artist will be trying to preserve the integrity of his own art, and he will defend his own artistic vision within the overall vision for the production.

There will be many, many compromises made throughout the production process. It should appear to the audience, however, that the production is the work of one single (and notably single-minded) theatrical artist. It falls to the director to ensure that his overall vision for artistic unity is maintained in every aspect of the production. For this reason, it is imperative that the director have a well-defined concept for the production, and that he be able to express that vision clearly and unambiguously to every member of his production team.

Effective communication is essential for a successful collaboration. Effective communication is based on two principles: (1) a willingness of each member of the production staff to enter fully and freely into the discussions and (2) a sensitivity of each member of the staff to other, sometimes diverse or contradictory interpretations of the theatrical experience for which they share responsibility.

It is important for you to distinguish between real communication and a meaningless exchange of words. Do not be misled by the *illusion* of communication. Members of your production staff may appear to be communicating with you and with one another, when, in fact, they are simply expressing and espousing their own personal agendas in subtly different ways. Words are exchanged, seemingly for good cause, but the participants may not be listening to what others are saying. A test of real communication lies in the ability of those involved in a discussion to reiterate clearly, in their own words, what is being said to them. Unless each member of the production staff can rephrase or restate what is being said, he is not truly participating in the discussion. Be aware of the effective level of communication in all your dealings with your design staff. The collaborative process is difficult, and without open communication, the production will surely fail.

The purpose of design meetings is to exchange relevant information regarding the artistic components of the production. This process may be formal or informal, structured or unstructured, one-on-one with individual designers or as a group. In your meetings you should strive to accomplish four objectives: (1) distribute and exchange information; (2) offer each member of the production team an opportunity to present his views, ask questions, or discuss any design elements of the production; (3) clarify all points of discussion, and (4) respond to any problems or challenges facing any relevant aspect of the production.

To communicate with your designers you must, first, be speaking the same language. Few directors today are wholly conversant in the language of design and technical theatre. Learn as much as you can about the design process before you attempt to hold your first design meeting. Study the history of costume and set design. Study the concepts and principles of designing for the stage—sets, costumes, lights, props, sound. Become familiar with the materials used in each discipline. Learn the basic terminology.

If you are ignorant of the principles and practice of design, you will be at a considerable disadvantage throughout the design and production process. Part of your responsibility in unifying the production is to understand *all* the elements that contribute to the realization of that objective.

What follows is a rough schedule of design meetings, leading to completed designs for the production.

FIRST DESIGN MEETING

This should be a group meeting. In this first meeting, you will do most of the talking. Greet everyone, make any necessary introductions, then get down to business and explain your overall concept for the production. With the designers, you will explore design options and possibilities and come to some agreement (at least in principle) about the conceptual and visual directions the production will take.

Your designers will want to know your thoughts in two important areas: (1) design elements—line, color, mass, balance, texture, composition—and (2) style—naturalistic, realistic, impressionistic, expressionistic, or any other "-istic" frame of reference appropriate to the production.

Use whatever means you can to convey your concept to your designers. Refer to drawings, paintings, photographs, architectural forms, music, poetry, rough sketches or models, even colors and shapes. Your designers will welcome any concrete frames of reference from which they can develop their own ideas. Some few designers may feel that this is an intrusion on their personal artistic domain or that it imposes unwelcome restrictions on their creativity. They'll get over it. It's your responsibility to provide guidelines and to impose some limitations on your designers' work, while at the same time allowing your designers the greatest possible artistic freedom within those limitations.

The designers may also want to explore an overall *metaphor* for the play, which you should also be prepared to discuss. Many designers have been trained to rely on a metaphor as the unifying factor in their individual designs, as well as the guiding principle for the overall production. The metaphor is a means of achieving production unity through a clear, specific, and consistent *visual* image—something that encapsulates, synthesizes, or otherwise represents the "world" of the play. "A crazy-quilt, topsy-turvy world," "a postatomic holocaust nightmare," and "an old, faded family photograph" are examples of metaphorical images that designers can readily grasp and translate into their work.

An important consideration in your discussions with your designers revolves around the differences in the *interpretation* of your vision for the production. As director, you are concerned primarily with the *conceptual* interpretation of the script—the essential elements of the plot, characterization, and theme. The designers are concerned with the *visual* interpretations of the script—of expressing the overall concept (or metaphor) of the production through the set, lighting, props, and costumes. The director remarks, *This is what I want to* say *with this production.* The designer responds, *This is how I want the production to* look. These are totally different approaches: concepts and visual images, though highly interdependent in a theatrical production, are definitely not the same thing. Concepts are thoughts, ideas, visions, and abstractions. These concepts must be brought to life through the physical elements of the production. That's what the designers do.

Invite questions from your designers throughout the process. Designers will often challenge your interpretation of the play to help clarify your vision in their own mind. The focus of any discussion with your designers should be on releasing and emphasizing the story line and the characters by visual means. Avoid specifics in the first design meeting, however, and avoid overanalyzing the script or any one particular element of it.

Ensure that each designer understands, and is able to articulate his understanding of your concept for the production and that there is general agreement to proceed along the same conceptual lines. Unless and until everyone on your design team buys into your concept or vision for the production, you cannot proceed together to realize that concept.

By the end of the first meeting, the designers should feel *empowered* by you to pursue whatever ideas they may have about the production and to follow whatever direction their individual designs will take, within the limitations you have imposed. Encourage them to give free rein to their imaginations and to explore their ideas as creatively and imaginatively as they can. Not much will be accomplished in this first meeting with regard to actual designs. Until the designers have produced something tangible, there is nothing more to discuss.

Before you dismiss the meeting, ask the designers to meet with you individually, preferably within a few days, to present their ideas and *rough* sketches and drawings, perhaps a rough model of the set, some *preliminary* choices of fabric, colors, and so on.

SECOND DESIGN MEETING

During the second design meeting, which is held with each designer individually, you will review the designer's work. Discuss the design elements, again in generalities. Discuss few specifics, except as required for clarification of your concept for the production. Listen closely, ask questions, and try to understand the direction that the designer is going. Think of this process as a collaboration. You and the designer need to work together to effect the best possible realization of your vision.

When necessary, reconcile the designer's ideas and preliminary designs with your concept for the production. Otherwise, allow the designer as much freedom as possible to explore his own ideas. The objective for this meeting is to come to some agreement regarding the direction that the designs will take.

It is your responsibility to make sure that all your designers are going in relatively the same direction toward your vision for the production. In many cases, this will involve a certain degree of tact, even with designers who have a good working relationship. You do not want to appear to favor one designer's ideas over another's. It's important that you encourage those ideas that best support your concept and those that contribute most directly to a unified style and approach in the designs.

Design discussions should be conducted in an environment of mutual understanding and respect—their understanding and respect of you and your concept for the production, and your understanding and respect of them and their abilities to realize that concept through their designs. It is not necessary to grovel at the feet of your designers, nor is it necessary to dictate their designs to them. Tact and diplomacy will accomplish much more than either an overly submissive or an unnecessarily dictatorial attitude.

Schedule the next meeting, preferably to occur in one week or less. Ask the designers to explore your suggestions further, and to come back to you in your next meeting with more ideas and revised designs.

THIRD DESIGN MEETING

Discuss the designs in detail at this meeting, with all designers present. Reconcile the designs with your concept. Come to an agreement about the final direction the designs will take. This may be the last opportunity you will have to make any substantive modifications of the designs. From this point, anything other than minor changes will severely disrupt the design process. You may have to start all over, an unwelcome proposition for everyone.

Then ask the designers to proceed to final designs and schedule a meeting, within the designers' time frames, by which all the designs will be complete.

FOURTH DESIGN MEETING

With all designers in attendance, discuss the final designs, in specifics. Relate all elements of the design to your overall concept for the production. If you agree with a designer on the final design, give the go-ahead for implementing them. If you and a designer are *not* in agreement, discuss specific changes and arrange to meet again for the go-ahead.

As the design meetings progress, you and your designers will discuss increasingly more detailed and technical aspects of the designs. You will spend a great deal more time discussing specific elements of the designs than exploring "style," "concepts," "images," and "metaphors." This is as it should be. The design process, like any other aspect of the production, progresses from the general to the specific, from the initial concept to the concrete realization of that concept.

FUTURE MEETINGS

For all subsequent meetings and communications with your design and technical staff, you will get significantly more accomplished, no matter the objective for the meeting, if you follow a few simple time-and-energy-saving techniques:

1. Rely on short conversations rather than formal meetings to exchange information or to resolve design matters. A formal meeting needs to be scheduled and a meeting place needs to be arranged. Time needs to be taken from two (or more) already busy schedules to accommodate what can probably be accomplished in two minutes in the hallway on the way to rehearsal.

2. Avoid scheduling a meeting around a meal. Little or nothing of consequence will be accomplished. Have the meeting first, then eat. You will get more done, in less time, in a meeting scheduled before a meal, rather than one scheduled after or during a meal. (A hungry meeting is a short meeting.)

3. If a formal meeting must be scheduled, set a specific time limit for the meeting and stick to it. Meetings always seem to take the amount of time allotted. Decide how much time a meeting *should* take, and cut the time in half. When the time is up, no matter where you are in the discussion, dismiss the meeting. You will need to do this only once or twice for your staff to get the message. Your people will stick closely to the point if they realize that they have only a finite amount of time to present their ideas and pursue solutions to pressing problems.

4. Handle each piece of paper that crosses your desk only once. Note your response on the original, and return it promptly to the sender or file it away. If record keeping is necessary, make a photocopy before you return the original to the sender.

5. If you have extra work to do, go to the theatre early rather than stay late. Schedule meetings and extra time with designers (and with actors) before rehearsals, not after. Much more will be accomplished when you are fresh and awake than if you put off extra work until you're mentally and physically exhausted. There will also be fewer distractions if you go to the theatre early, and you won't be tempted to skip the work and go out for pizza instead. You are also much more likely to stick to the point of the discussion if you know you have to leave to get to a scheduled rehearsal.

6. The greatest time-and-energy-saving technique you can employ is to hire the best people you can find, delegate to them as much responsibility as you possibly can, and trust them to do the work. Practice a policy of noninterference. Good people will do good work if you let them. Stay informed of their progress. Drop by to see how they're doing. Praise and encourage them. Otherwise, leave them alone to do what you hired them to do.

Rehearsal and Production Management | 4

Cast Management

*E*very actor, no matter how great or small the role, should be made to feel an invaluable and indispensable part of the production, vital to every scene in which she appears. Nevertheless, she must also understand that no actor is more important than any other, nor is any actor more important that the production as a whole. Actors must recognize that the integrity of the production will not be compromised or sacrificed for the sake of one person.

As the director, you set the example for expected behavior throughout the production company, but most particularly for your cast. If you arrive early for rehearsals, well prepared, cheerful, and enthusiastic, so will your cast. If you wander into rehearsal late, ill prepared, sullen, and uncommunicative, you can expect similar behavior from your cast.

Directors are sometimes at a loss what to expect from their actors. They don't want to expect too much and risk alienating them, nor do they want to expect too little and fall short of a good production. You can reasonably expect that your actors will:

1. Be familiar with the rehearsal schedule and attend all scheduled rehearsals at which their presence and participation is required.

2. Arrive on time to all rehearsals and performance calls, costume fittings, and other appointments.
3. Be prepared for rehearsal, meaning they will be familiar with the scene, will have learned all their lines by the time required, and will bring their script and a pencil to all rehearsals.
4. Be prepared and in place for all entrances, whether in rehearsal or in performance.
5. Not distract other actors, nor cause any distraction or disturbance during rehearsals and performances.
6. Be actively involved in rehearsals and the production and in the betterment of themselves and their art.

These guidelines are not particularly demanding. You should expect that any actor who enters the rehearsal hall accepts these very basic "conditions of employment." Establish some early ground rules regarding rehearsal behavior, and do not allow any actor to demean another or to behave disrespectfully toward another actor or toward you. Essentially, cast management is based on respect for the art, respect for oneself, and respect for one another.

The making of theatre should be a joy, not an ordeal. Maintain an overriding sense of enthusiasm and commitment, and encourage a dedicated effort toward a mutually rewarding and enriching experience. Endeavor to build a sense of trust, understanding, and mutual respect between your cast and you from the very beginning. Within that kind of supportive environment, your cast management problems will be few.

THE RECALCITRANT ACTOR

Occasionally you will encounter an actor who refuses to take direction, fights you every step of the way, or reluctantly accepts your direction only to change it later. Likewise, an actor may treat you or other cast members disrespectfully or may seem otherwise incapable of fulfilling his responsibilities to the production. If you feel it is detrimental to the other actors or to the production to allow an actor to remain with the company, and if you feel that any efforts to resolve the problem would be futile, you should replace her at the earliest possible opportunity.

Nothing is ever that simple, of course, particularly when dealing with living, breathing human beings. Replacing an actor is always disruptive, no matter when or how you do it. The negative effect is lessened the earlier it comes in the rehearsal period, but there *is* a negative effect nevertheless.

Every actor knows, somewhere in the back of her mind, that she can be replaced, but it is an abstraction. No actor ever believes it will happen, certainly not to her. The dismissal of an actor happens so rarely that when it *does* happen, it brings the abstraction clearly into the realm of possibility: *If it happened to her, it can happen to me.* You need to be prepared for the temporary sense of insecurity and unrest that replacing an actor engenders.

If you must replace an actor, and are able to do so, then *do* it, and do it early in the rehearsal process. The longer the problem continues, the greater its detrimental effect on the cast and on the production. No one should endure abusive, disrespectful, or irresponsible behavior. Advise the replacements or understudies, adjust the rehearsal schedule as necessary, and carry on. The cast will pull together. The longer you wait, the harder it will be for you and for the remaining members of the cast: no matter how actors feel about one another personally, they nevertheless invest in one another.

If you have no replacement or if it's too late in the rehearsal period or if the offending party is the producer's son or daughter, then you have a problem. Somehow, you've got to minimize the negative effect this person is having on the show. This isn't easy. If you are aware of the problem, everyone else probably is too. Nothing stays a secret in a theatrical production company for very long. (In fact, you will be the *last* to know when difficulties arise within the company. It's not that the cast is reluctant to tell you or that they are being secretive but that they think you already know. After all, you're the director; you know everything.) Work privately with the problem actor to resolve the situation as best you can.

The Problem Director

If *you're* the problem, that's another matter altogether. You may sense that you—your methods, your personality, your "style"—are the cause of growing resentment, resistance, or unrest in the cast.

If you feel you can talk to members of the cast objectively, privately ask for their comments and observations. Ask a colleague to sit in on rehearsals and comment on your interaction with the cast. If you feel you need to change your attitude or approach for the betterment of the production, do the best you can to do so.

By no means should you change any aspect of your directing solely for interpersonal reasons. Those should be addressed one on one, not aired in front of the company. That serves no purpose other than to fragment the company. Sides will be taken. Factions will be joined. Ultimately, the production will suffer.

Resist becoming personally involved with any of your actors on an emotional or romantic level during the production. No matter how objective you feel you can remain or how discreet you think you can be about your relationship, some small measure of subjectivity will creep into what should be an otherwise objective actor-director relationship. Other members of the cast will notice even the slightest difference in approach that you use with one or more of them and may come to resent this special treatment. You will have your favorites, of course, but do your best to balance praise and criticism among all the members of the cast, and treat all of them with equal respect and consideration.

LINES OF COMMUNICATION

Use your assistant director and stage manager as buffers between you and the acting company. The purpose is not to insulate you or to isolate you from the actors, but to avoid unnecessary distractions, particularly during times of intense concentration. Actors will ask the strangest things, usually at the most inopportune times. Let it be understood early in the rehearsal period that all questions that cannot be directed to you from the stage during rehearsals are to be addressed to the assistant director or the stage manager, who will in turn speak to you if he feels the problem warrants your attention. (Empower the stage manager and your assistant director to resolve any minor concerns on their own.) This keeps the lines of communication open between you and the cast during rehearsals but limits opportunities for actors and others to engage you in discussions about matters unrelated to the task at hand.

OPEN VERSUS CLOSED REHEARSALS

It seems apparent that rehearsals should be closed to all but those directly involved. Few artists in any other medium—painters, for instance, or composers—allow anyone, including close friends and relatives, to look over their shoulder while they're working. It's distracting. It interferes with the artist's concentration. It imposes unwelcome elements into the environment and on the work. It invites comments, questions, and judgments. It implies that the observer, by being allowed to view the work, somehow becomes part of the artistic endeavor.

Nontheatre people don't understand the production process, and even theatre people may misinterpret what they observe. Those who watch a single rehearsal (or only a few minutes of a rehearsal) witness only a very small portion of the total production process. The occasional rehearsal watcher has no real idea of what came before or what is to follow, yet she feels obligated to comment on the process, to give "helpful" hints to the actors and director, and to make judgments about the entire production.

A rehearsal is not a free show. It's an artistic work in progress. Until opening night, the theatre is an artist's studio. It is (or should be) the private domain of the theatre artists who inhabit it—the actors, director, and designers—who rightly deserve respect and utmost consideration in their work, as artists and as individuals. Artists work alone, until it is time, *by the artist's reckoning,* for the general public to participate in the artistic experience.

Only those directly involved with a production should be allowed to attend working rehearsals and only for legitimate reasons directly related to the production. Refuse all requests for friends and relatives of the cast and crew to sit in on a rehearsal. If you make even one exception, expect a flood of requests to follow. Instruct your stage manager to refuse these requests from visitors who appear at the stage door and politely and tactfully to "redirect" anyone who inadvertently wanders into the theatre during a rehearsal.

Under no circumstances should you allow anyone other than the cast, crew, and designers to attend a technical rehearsal. The same applies to orchestra rehearsals for musicals. (Be sure your music director and the musicians understand this as well.)

You may ruffle some feathers with this no-visitors policy. It may be a tradition in your organization that rehearsal watchers are welcome to drop in at any time. As usual, there may be political considerations. You may have to balance political expediency with practical concerns in attempting to implement a new rehearsal policy. Tact, diplomacy, and a competent stage manager should see you through the more trying times.

If you feel comfortable that the show is in *great* (not just good) shape, and if you foresee no problems in doing so, you may wish to invite the theatre staff (who might otherwise not see the performance at all), those who were disenfranchised by your no-visitor policy, or a small student audience for the final dress rehearsal. Students should be accompanied by an instructor, if appropriate to their age, and any invited audience should conduct themselves as if they were attending a regularly scheduled performance. Allow no disrespect to the actors or to the production. No talking, no disruptions or distractions, no overly enthusiastic displays for friends or relatives onstage, no wandering around the theatre. (This is not a movie.) If you have any problems, immediately clear the theatre.

UNDERSTUDY AND REPLACEMENT REHEARSALS

In the professional theatre, understudy rehearsals are generally conducted by the stage manager. Replacement rehearsals, except for minor roles, are generally conducted by the director.

The difference between an understudy and a replacement is that an understudy has likely been with the production from its inception, is intimately familiar with it, has a good idea of the staging and interpretation of the play, and can readily fit in, even on very short notice. A replacement most likely comes from outside the cast, has little or no idea about the staging or interpretation of the play, and needs to be gradually assimilated into the production, if on an accelerated schedule. The replacement needs to *learn* the show. The understudy needs only to *reinforce* certain aspects of the production with which she is already familiar.

Directors of amateur productions seem reluctant to entrust their work to others, even to a highly competent stage manager or assistant director. Perhaps the work was hard won. Perhaps the director is obsessive or insecure. Whatever the reason, in the amateur theatre the director usually conducts both replacement and understudy rehearsals.

DRESSING ROOMS

In assigning dressing rooms, do the best you can to balance the needs of the individual actors and actresses with the needs of the production.

It is general practice to put the extras or chorus together in two large dressing rooms, one for men, one for women. Group the bit players and supporting players as equitably as possible, taking into account the personalities of the actors, character groupings, and so on. The women are placed closer to the stage than the men at each level of the onstage hierarchy, and those involved with quick costume changes are placed closest to the stage of all, no matter their relative rank.

The biggest challenge you will face with dressing room assignments will be with the leading players and the not-quite-leading players. Unless there is a true star of the show, no one actor or actress should have a private dressing room. If a private, quick-change room is necessary, set aside a separate dressing room or off-stage area for that purpose only. It should be not become any one actor's private domain.

One good thing about the limited dressing room space often found in amateur theatre performance venues—one dressing room for the ladies, the other for the men—is that it eliminates the problem of assigning dressing rooms, other than, *Men here, ladies there.* The actors will stake out their own territory in the dressing room, and work out the onstage hierarchy amongst themselves, thereby relieving you of this sometimes troublesome responsibility.

THE CURTAIN CALL

The cardinal rules for a curtain call are (1) keep it short, (2) keep moving, (3) keep building, (4) keep smiling, and (5) get off the stage. Unless purposefully done in character for stylistic purposes—as might be done in a Moliere play, for instance—the actors should take the curtain call, not the characters. The play is over. The characters no longer exist.

Consider waiting to block the curtain call until the end of the last run-through before technical and dress rehearsals. This gives you time to determine the best order for the curtain call, to decide on the groupings of the actors, and so on. It also gives the company something to look forward to, as the true culmination of rehearsals. For the cast, the rehearsal period isn't really over, the show isn't really done, until the curtain call has been blocked.

Generally speaking, the script dictates the order of the actors in the curtain call—least important characters to most important. Sometimes this is difficult to determine on paper, but it should become clear to you during rehearsals.

For a standard curtain call, group all the extras together—those with no lines and/or other distinguishing characteristics—and bring them on for a bow first. Next come the bit players—walk-ons, those with one or two lines and/or running gags—again all together. Following them are the supporting players, in groups of two, three, or four related characters. Bring on the leading players last, giving each a solo turn. If the lead is shared, as in *Romeo and Juliet,* for example, bring the two actors on together, each indicating a solo turn for the other. The company as a whole then takes one final bow.

As for arranging particular groupings, you may find the actors will sort this out very nicely by themselves. If necessary, you can always step in later, "to adjust the stage picture." (Adjusting the stage picture is always an acceptable reason for change.)

Not everyone will be pleased with the final order of the curtain call. Under no circumstances, however, should you change the curtain call to please an actor or to assuage her bruised ego. It's not an actor's place to argue with you about the curtain call, nor should you compromise your position and authority by engaging in an argument or discussion about it. Explain the order of the curtain call, if you must, and let it go at that.

In amateur productions, you may find that audience applause for a particular actor is occasionally in direct contrast to the quality of his performance. Audiences seem to respond more to apparent "effort" than to true artistry. A cute bit player may elicit considerably more applause than a very competent leading player. (Leading ladies who cry or die onstage also seem to elicit a disproportionate amount of applause.) If you sense that this may be the case for your production, you can remedy the situation in different ways:

1. Assemble the entire cast on stage for the curtain call, and have them do *only* a company bow. Audience members will applaud their favorites in their own minds, but the entire company will benefit from the overall response.
2. Arrange the cast into large groups of related characters, and have each *group* take a bow together.
3. Put the audience favorite in a small group of featured players—a group of three actors works best. The effect is the same as the company bow, but on a smaller scale.

As an example, let's block the curtain call for *Romeo and Juliet,* a show with a large cast.

Put the Capulets and their allies together—Juliet, Capulet, Lady Capulet, Nurse, Paris, Tybalt, and their servants and friends; put the Montagues and their allies together—Romeo, Montague, Lady Montague, Mercutio, Benvolio, servants and friends; and put everybody else—Prince, Chorus, Friar Lawrence, Apothecary, citizens of Verona, and beggars and thieves of indeterminate lineage—together in a third group. Have the entire cast on stage at the beginning of the curtain call. First, have the "everybody else" group bow together. Then the Montagues, followed by the Capulets (or vice versa). If you like, have the star-crossed lovers step forward for their own bows, separately and together (or together then separately). Finally, bring the entire company together, literally as well as symbolically, and give the audience a final company bow, led by the actors playing Romeo and Juliet.

This arrangement avoids the awkward and sometimes embarrassing rise and fall of applause through the lengthy parade of players. Mercutio (although he exits the play early) is generally more popular with an audience than Tybalt (if they even remember who he is), more popular certainly than Paris (a thankless role), and occasionally even more popular than Romeo. Juliet invariably elicits more applause than Romeo (unless Romeo is a star, and Juliet is not), and very often the Nurse is more popular than anybody. By grouping the cast by households, the audience response is spread more evenly among the actors, leaving only Romeo and Juliet to sort it out between themselves.

Plan your curtain call carefully. Even "spontaneous" displays, like presenting flowers to the leading lady or calling the director onstage for a bow, should be planned. Prepare (and rehearse) anything like this within the existing curtain call format.

Don't change the curtain call once it is blocked and set. Ignore the audience's exuberant shouting, whistling, and foot stamping. Likewise, ignore shouts of "Bravo!" and "Author!" (No one ever shouts "Director!") Do the curtain call as blocked, fade the lights, drop the curtain, bring up the house lights, and go home. Let the sound of the tumultuous applause ring in your ears, but don't let it go to your head.

PHOTO CALLS

Arrangements for publicity photos should be made as early in the rehearsal period as possible, even if there is no set, no costumes, and no real idea of what the actors will look like on stage for the finished performance. Confer with the costumer and set designer, and put together an appropriate "look" for the photographs that will best represent the production. Use as few actors as possible for these photographs—two or three leading players should be sufficient.

There is no "good" time for a full-cast photo call. Think of all the times when you *could* schedule a photo call, and you will find some negative aspect to each of them. After dress rehearsal? It's late, everybody is tired, and you want the cast to get a good night's sleep before opening night. Before dress rehearsal? Too hectic. There are also likely to be scheduling problems with one or more members of the cast, even if the photo call is clearly noted on the rehearsal schedule. People have jobs, families, other commitments. After the show on opening night? Think about it. Would you like to make your friends and relatives in the audience wait around for the next hour or so while you and everyone else in the cast has their picture taken?

A possible solution is to schedule the photo call on a weekend afternoon prior to an evening performance. The cast should be refreshed and relaxed, and there will be enough time for the technical staff and the costume and makeup crews to prepare for the shoot. The photo call can progress unhurriedly and in relatively good humor. You might arrange for food to be brought to the theatre—a picnic menu or pizza—after the photo call is over. The food will be consumed well in advance of the performance, and the cast will be already assembled at the theatre, in a good mood and up for the evening performance.

If the only time you can schedule a photo call is after a rehearsal or a performance, get together with your stage manager to decide the shots you want, in what order. The photo call will proceed much more efficiently if you work *backward* from the end of the show. Shoot the curtain call first (the cast is already in costume), then the last scene, and so on, back to the beginning. Post a list with the exact lines or stage business appropriate for each shot, so the cast knows the order of the shots and can change costumes or otherwise prepare for one shot while another is being staged. Make sure the technical staff also has a list so that they can prepare the lights, change the set, and provide other technical support for each shot as needed. Simplify the procedure by requiring minimal costume and set changes.

Photos may be taken during one of the *first* dress rehearsals, but only if you feel the photographer will not unduly distract the actors and if there is no audience. Ask the photographer to be quiet and unobtrusive and to stay in the auditorium or in the wings; he should never be allowed onto the set. Tell the actors about the photographer's presence in advance, of course, and expect a slightly diminished level of performance. No matter how unobtrusive the photographer may be, the actors will still be distracted.

DEATH, ACCIDENTS, AND ILLNESS

Deaths and serious accidents and illnesses unfortunately do occur, if rarely, within the course of preparation for a production. If something like this does affect one or more members of your production company, either directly or indirectly, the primary concern should be the physical and emotional well-being of the individual(s) involved.

A production company is its own small community, composed of real people, with real thoughts and feelings. Every member of the community will be affected, to a greater or lesser extent, by any unfortunate circumstance or occurrence relating to one of their number. A play or a musical is only one aspect of life, albeit an important one to theatre people. The importance of life and the quality of that life far exceed the importance of any element of the production.

An important secondary concern is the well-being of the production. This usually revolves around the age-old adage, "The show must go on." The producing organization needs to determine if the show must go on or not. There will be those inside and outside of your theatre community who will ask, *Why* must the show go on? You will need a good answer. It's not a matter of what the people involved in the unfortunate circumstance may have wanted. It's not a matter of precedent or budgetary considerations or "doing what you're paid for." It's about people. It's a matter of fulfilling the needs of the community, in this case the needs of the production community. In some instances, it's also a matter of healing, of reinforcing a sense of continuance, or of providing a fitting memorial. Whatever the reason, it should be one that responds to the needs of the people in the production community.

Every member of the production community should be consulted. Each person will not necessarily "vote" on the outcome (a theatre organization is not a democracy), but each should feel that he or she had a *voice* in the decision. Few members of the organization will vote to cancel the production. Some may wish to set back the opening a week or two, or otherwise provide for a short period of adjustment. One factor to consider in the decision is that unless the incident occurred within only a few days of the opening, most people will *expect* to follow the same schedule, for the simple reason that they have been trained to believe, for better or for worse, that "the show must go on."

Very few productions have ever been canceled, even for the death of a director or cast member. Openings may need to be rescheduled, but the production community usually finds some way to pull together and fill the void left by departed friends and colleagues. It is a remarkable ability, and one that should not be taken lightly.

As the director, you must be concerned with practical as well as personal matters. You carry a responsibility to every member of your production company to support what you feel would be in her or his best interests relative to the production as a whole. Practically speaking, whether or not it has been determined that the show will go on, understudies and replacements should be notified as soon as possible, should their services be needed. You will also need to meet with your design and technical personnel to determine what changes, if any, are needed in the production schedule. If you're directing a musical, you will need to consult your music director and choreographer about changes or adjustments to the rehearsal schedule and changes in the cast.

Whatever the situation, take care of the people first.

REHEARSAL NOTES

Perhaps more time has been wasted in giving rehearsal notes than in any other part of the production process. Whenever possible, write your rehearsal notes legibly and distribute them to the actors (or post them) before the next scheduled rehearsal. The actors are quite capable of reading and understanding these notes on their own. Give notes orally only if they deal with lengthy and complex matters involving most or all of the cast, or if you are addressing the problems or concerns of individual actors. It is common courtesy not to giving potentially embarrassing notes to an actor in front of other members of the cast.

Remember to include some flattering or encouraging remarks to the actors and technical staff in your notes. Mention not only what went wrong, but also some of what went right.

An example of the extremes to which directors will sometimes go involves a director I once knew, who would tape-record his often lengthy notes while a rehearsal was underway. Afterward, he would call the cast together, rewind the tape, and replay the taped notes, stopping the tape after each note. He would then repeat the note, often in the same words he'd used on the tape, and "explain" the note, sometimes taking several minutes to do so. The note session frequently lasted longer than the rehearsal!

If you prefer to give oral notes to your cast after rehearsals, do it quickly. Say what you have to say, and say it clearly. Ask the actor if he understands. If the answer is yes, move on. If the answer is no, give a *brief* explanation. If the actor still doesn't understand, arrange to meet individually later.

Production Management

It is commonly thought that the director's job is finished once the production opens. In some cases that may be true, but in many cases it is not. Your responsibilities change after opening night, but it is more a change in focus or emphasis than a complete change of government. Whereas throughout the rehearsal process your emphasis was on developing your vision for the production, your focus after opening night is to ensure the continuance of that vision.

In a professional theatre organization this responsibility is entrusted, for the most part, to the stage manager. The director may watch a performance or two and give a few notes, but often she is off on her next directing assignment right after opening night, possibly in another part of the country. This is unfortunate, but it is often unavoidable. It is not reasonable to expect a director to devote several weeks or months (possibly even years) of her life to a single long-running show, simply to be there as emotional support for the cast and crew or to make sure the cast continues to perform the show as directed.

This does not entirely relieve the professional director of a responsibility to the production. She may return periodically to watch the show, to assure continuity, give a few notes, make a few appropriate changes, or take out the "improvements." If there are cast replacements, particularly in the leading roles, the director may supervise rehearsals for the new cast member. Again, this may not always be possible, and the stage manager may rehearse cast replacements.

At the professional level, the cast and crew are expected to perform the show as it was originally directed, even over a long run, even in the absence of the director's guiding hand. In amateur organizations, however, the director often remains with the production through the run of the show, and in some instances she may attend every performance. In small amateur organizations, the director may assume a backstage role once the show opens, on the running crew, perhaps, or as a security blanket for an inexperienced cast and/or crew. This gives the director something to do besides stand at the back of the theatre and fret, and it makes her available if anything during the performance requires a quick decision or her physical assistance.

If the director of an amateur production suddenly disappears after weeks of constantly being there, some members of the cast may feel abandoned. These insecurities may manifest themselves in tentative performances and in tensions among members of the cast and crew. Then, too, one or two members of the cast may feel that they can now give the performance they've always wanted to give, not necessarily the one they've been directed to give. This can be detrimental to the production and very disconcerting to the other cast members. Therefore, you must turn the show over to the cast and crew without abdicating your continuing responsibility to them or to the production. Your presence must be felt, even in your seeming absence.

This is as much a matter of attitude and the cast-director relationship you have developed throughout the rehearsal period as it is your physical presence in the theatre for every performance. The cast must trust by now that you have done your best to make them look good, and you must trust them to carry out their responsibilities to you, to the production, and to each other.

PERFORMANCE NOTES

If the run is short, give notes for each performance. Post the general cast notes and give notes to individual actors privately prior to the next performance. Mention some of the things that went particularly well, in addition to the small problems and changes. If you must meet with the cast as whole, schedule an early call for the next day rather than hold everyone after a performance.

Confer privately with designers or technicians. There is no need for your cast to spend their time reading technical notes that are of no concern to them.

If the run is long, give notes for the first few performances, then only on as needed through the balance of the run. Post an occasional

Doing great! or *Terrific show last night!* to keep spirits up and to let the cast know that you're still out there.

Second-Night Letdown

The first night was great. Great performance. Great audience. Everything was terrific. Couldn't have been better.

The second night is awful. Timing is off. Energy is down. The actors wait for the big laughs of opening night, but they never come. The harder the actors try, the worse it gets. The audience just sits there. It's a relief when the final curtain falls.

What happened? How can one performance be so different from another?

The human mind learns through mistakes—otherwise known as trial and error—and by comparisons. On the second night, the actors had no basis for comparison. They did exactly the same things they did on opening night, thinking that the second-night audience would react in the same places and in the same ways the opening-night audience did. They were wrong. What worked on opening night didn't work on the second night.

By the third performance, however, the actors will have learned to adjust and adapt their performance to the new situation, and to the new audience. They will have made many of these necessary adjustments and adaptations without being consciously aware of them. After the second night the cast will have been able to compare their first two performances and learn from the differences—something they couldn't do after only one performance. They made mistakes on the second night they won't make again on the third night. It is a confusing, frustrating, and painful learning experience for some, but they learn nevertheless.

Is there a way to avoid second-night letdown? Yes and no. There is a way to lessen the effect of the letdown (and minimize the mistakes), but there is no consistently successful way to eliminate it.

The point is, you can prepare your actors for what is about to happen to them, even if you can't really do anything about it. Explain to the cast *what* happens, and *why* it happens. Explain to them what they can expect out there. Don't scare them to death, of course, but do try to heighten their awareness. Mention to them that the audience will *not* laugh in all the same places they did on opening night, so they shouldn't wait for laughs that may never come. Tell them to stay awake and aware, to adjust to the audience as they go along, without expectations or preconceptions.

Above all, caution them against blaming the second-night audience for having different reactions. Remind them that their relationship with the audience is not adversarial. They and the audience are in this *together*. Tonight's audience has no idea what last night's audience did, so they can't be held accountable for not reacting the same way—the way that you think they're *supposed* to react because that's what the *first* night's audience did.

Two additional things may help explain the second-night letdown. First, most of the actors have given absolutely no thought to any performance past opening night. It may come as a shock to some that there *is* a second performance, and a third, and so on. Second, the actors have been geared up for that first big performance—that magical opening night. Now that it has come and gone, they're somewhat at a loss. They were probably up too late, and now they're a little tired. Emotionally, they're not as up as they were yesterday. They should be, but they're not. They may seem a little distant from the tasks that lie before them, a little distracted, perhaps, particularly compared with the total physical, mental, and emotional involvement that they experienced on the night before.

It falls to you to do what you can to get the cast back into it. A rousing pregame speech may help. Praise the opening night performance. Encourage the cast to rekindle some of that opening night feeling, the enthusiasm, the involvement, the energy, the excitement.

Now, the tricks of the trade: change a few things. There are probably a few things that need to be changed anyway, so it shouldn't be too difficult to find some bit of blocking or a line or two that needs a small adjustment. Move an actor's entrance up ever so slightly, or put it back a little. Change a bit of business. Small things. Little changes. Don't do anything that will upset the overall flow of the show. Spread the changes around the cast, and try to choose things that will affect the most people at some point during the performance.

Don't rehearse the changes. Tell the cast what the changes are, and let them fend for themselves. The idea is to give the actors something to think about during the performance besides the audience, something that will put their focus back on stage where it belongs. By spreading the changes throughout the performance and throughout the cast, you will keep everyone on stage interested and aware from the opening curtain to the curtain call.

Call it psychology. Call it manipulation. Call it whatever you like. It works, and it helps minimize the second-night letdown, which is the point.

It is unlikely that your technical crew will suffer the same second-night letdown that the cast does. Their work does not depend on audience reaction, for instance, or other intangibles, like their emotional state. Still, it couldn't hurt to buck up the technical crew just a little. Make the rounds backstage. Let your technical crew know that you're thinking about them, that you know they're there, and that you appreciate their work. You don't want them to become lax or complacent simply because they're competent. Praise their competence, and encourage their continued improvement at the same time.

Pickup/Brushup Rehearsals

A show that runs every night but Monday and twice on Sunday very likely doesn't need brushup or pickup rehearsals. Shows that run only on weekends or have several days between performances will benefit from a refresher rehearsal every now and again, even if the run is relatively short.

A brushup rehearsal during a long run is usually called by the director in order to take out the "improvements" that have accrued along the way. Directors prefer to have the play performed the way they directed it, no matter how long the run or how creative the cast. They're funny that way.

Midrun Changes

As the director, you have the right to insist on changes at any point in the run of the play. Consider any substantial changes very carefully, however. If your production run is short, you should probably leave well enough alone. The production will not suffer appreciably. If there is a major problem, by all means fix it, but for the most part, ignore the small stuff.

In a long run, little problems generally have a way of working themselves out on their own. The production will grow and change over time. What once seemed a problem will have been gradually assimilated into the production and will become an integral part of it. If you would rather that didn't happen, then change it, of course. Remember, however, that any changes you make, large or small, will take time to settle in. Excessive changes will only disrupt or impede the growth of the production and will likely alienate those who have to implement the changes. At some point in the process, you need to let go. You need to let the production stand or fall on its own merits.

Postproduction Evaluation

It's an odd phenomenon, but most actors don't care to discuss a show, or to assess their performance in it, after the show has closed. The postperformance glow may last a day or two, but after that it's a dead issue. They're already involved in some other project, possibly in rehearsal for another show, and their minds are about a million miles away from last Saturday or Sunday night. It's over. Ancient history.

Any postproduction evaluation you do will most likely be with your department heads and the front office on the technical and financial aspects of the production. You can review with them what worked well (and not so well), what changes or adjustments should be made for future productions, and so on. You probably won't be telling your technical people anything they don't already know, but they will be pleased that you noticed, and they will respect you for your awareness and understanding of technical matters. If the show came in under budget (it happens), share the accolades of your producer and general manager with those who spent, or rather didn't spend, the money. If the show went over budget, accept the responsibility yourself. As a general principle, share praise and absorb blame.

If the show went well, great. Revel in the applause of the audience and the good will of your colleagues while you can. In another week or so, no one will mention it. Success in the theatre is fleeting.

If the show wasn't so great, well, sometimes the magic works, and sometimes it doesn't. You did your best. The cast and crew knocked themselves out. Yet, somehow, for some reason or another, the show didn't work. The critics hated it. The audience stayed away in droves. Life goes on. Learn what you can from the experience. Even if what you've learned is never to do that again, at least you've learned *something*.

You will learn more from the less successful productions you direct than from the over-the-top, sold-out, boffo hits. Few directors are blessed with the ability to do it right the first time and every time. Every director makes mistakes. The best directors are those who learn from their mistakes and who learn to avoid making the same mistakes in the future.

Success is the result of good judgment (and the occasional happy accident). Good judgment is the result of experience. What we call "experience" is often the result of bad judgment. It's how we learn.

Managing a   5
Musical

A musical is a tribute to theatrical art. A musical brings together three of the major performing arts—acting, music, and dance—and the fine arts of design, painting, and sculpture. Everything about a musical is larger than life. It is a triumph of the human spirit (and often of the human will and human endurance) when the diverse elements of a musical are brought together in a successful, unified production.

Directing a musical can be a wonderfully fulfilling experience, particularly when, as if by magic, it all falls together on opening night. Few experiences in the theatre compare to the excitement generated on opening night of a musical—the electric thrill of the first notes of the overture, "Curtain up!," and the exhilaration of the opening number. There is theatrical magic, of course, and there is also hard work. Directing a musical is a complex and extremely time-consuming, labor-intensive undertaking. A musical places considerable, sometimes overwhelming demands on the director and the producing organization. From a purely logistical standpoint, for instance, a musical production often involves a large cast, an orchestra, an enlarged artistic and technical staff, more-than-adequate rehearsal and performance facilities, increased production costs, increased publicity and promotion costs (to bring in more customers to offset the higher production costs), a longer rehearsal period, and above all, very careful planning.

The odds that you will one day be asked to direct a musical are great. If theatre is a business, musicals are "big business." It is a rare theatre organization that doesn't have at least one musical in its season, particularly those that rely on season subscriptions as their primary means of support. A successful musical can generate very considerable profits. In many instances, proceeds from the musical underwrite the cost of other productions on the schedule (a fact that you will hear repeatedly during budget negotiations). In more than a few cases, a musical production is the only reason some theatres are able to exist at all.

You can prepare for directing a musical by learning all you can about the process, reading books on the subject, perhaps even attaching yourself to a local theatre organization and shadowing the director through a musical production. Volunteer to serve as assistant director if you have the time, or otherwise offer to help out whenever you can. Observe the production process closely. It's much better to learn to direct a musical by working on several of them in other capacities first.

Prerehearsal Organization

Prerehearsal organization for a musical proceeds in much the same way as it does for a straight play, but on a much broader scale. Preproduction planning is the key. It is vital that as many matters as possible pertaining to the organization and management of a musical production be addressed *before* rehearsals start. Once they do, there will be little time for anything but the most pressing concerns.

The most important rule is this: delegate, delegate, delegate. If you don't delegate problem-solving authority to others, you will be besieged with one time-consuming problem after another. You won't have time to resolve all those problems and still direct the show. You also won't have time to be looking over everyone's shoulder, so empower others to resolve all but the most insurmountable or potentially disastrous problems on their own. You may be surprised to discover just how smoothly the production will run without your constant, finger-in-every-pie supervision.

PLAY SELECTION

The people who are going to *do* the show—the director, music director, choreographer, and designers—really ought to be the ones who choose it. Often, however, the choice lies with the producer, the producing organization, or the "musical selection committee." Occasionally, you may be able to suggest a particular musical or provide a range of musicals from which the producer, the producing organization, or the selection committee may choose. On very rare occasions, you may get to choose one yourself.

In the latter two circumstances, the first order of business is to meet with your music director, choreographer, and designers. Begin your research with the catalogs from rental agencies that supply musicals to theatre organizations. A catalog description rarely provides enough information on which to base a final decision, of course, but it can give you an idea of the overall requirements for a show—cast size, number of sets required, period in which the musical is set, size and composition of the orchestra, and similar information. Your production staff will no doubt be familiar with a wide range of musicals. Solicit their suggestions and advice.

Once you have a reasonable number of shows from which to make your final selection, you and every member of your production staff must read each script and review each musical score and determine the musical and staging requirements. A particular show may have terrific music and dance numbers but an insubstantial, dated, or otherwise inappropriate script. Another musical may have a great script and wonderful music but very few opportunities for dance numbers. These considerations will have to be weighed against your requirements.

Rental agencies will provide perusal copies of the script and score at a nominal fee, sometimes just the cost of postage. You might be able to find a copy of a script in the library, but you likely won't be able to find a copy of the score other than at a music store, in which case you will have to purchase it.

Apply for a royalty quotation at the same time you request perusal materials. You'll need that information later and asking for it now saves time later. (If you find that the royalty is exorbitant, by your standards, you can cross the musical off your list right away and explore other alternatives.)

There are recordings of many shows. Although they give you a good sense of the music in the show, they may vary widely from the actual stage production. The music for the dance numbers is invariably shortened or cut, for instance, and numbers are often rearranged or otherwise "adjusted," usually shortened.

Review the play selection criteria in Chapter 2, which also apply to choosing a musical. There are, of course, additional criteria, discussed below.

Types of Musicals ■ There is no "typical" musical. There is a wide range of types and styles of musicals from which to choose. The type of musical you finally choose to produce will be determined to a great extent by other considerations, such as your talent pool, technical facilities, and budget.

There are six basic types, each with its own characteristics and production requirements. Some musicals fit very neatly into one of these categories, others are a combination of one or more of them:

1. *The book musical.* Musicals like *Annie, Oklahoma!, West Side Story, My Fair Lady,* and *South Pacific* are based on a substantial and viable plot—a good, basic script with well-developed characters—and the music, dance, and drama are well integrated. The musical numbers are divided fairly equally among the leading players, and the chorus does more than provide "stage dressing" during the songs and dances. The actors in the leading roles must be equally talented in acting and singing, and the chorus must include strong singers and dancers.

2. *The star vehicle.* Some shows, like *Gypsy, Hello, Dolly!,* and *Sweet Charity* were originally written to showcase a particular performer's talents. Other shows, although not written for one specific performer, may also be termed a star vehicle because the show revolves around one particularly strong role, as in *A Funny Thing Happened on the Way to the Forum, Zorba,* or *Fiddler on the Roof.* This type of show requires a very strong leading performer who can carry the show from start to finish, has tremendous presence, and is a highly talented actor/singer, actor/dancer, or singer/dancer.

3. *The musical spectacular. Cats* and *Starlight Express* are examples of this type of show. If there *is* a book, it usually serves only as a framework on which to hang the music, dancing, lighting, costumes, or special effects. The "show," the spectacle, is the reason for its existence. The technical budget for such a musical can be quite substantial, which makes producing a spectacle show problematic for most amateur theatre organizations. There are also very considerable demands placed on the design and technical staff, as well as on the actual production facilities. If the necessary spectacle cannot be supported technically or budgetarily, the show cannot be done. No spectacle, no show.

4. *The ensemble musical.* Characteristics of an ensemble show include a relatively small cast, equal division of musical numbers, few or no chorus parts, minimal sets and costumes, few technical demands, and no spectacle. Consequently, ensemble shows generally require a smaller budget and minimal technical sup-

port. There are concerns other than budgetary, however. A small-cast, small-budget show necessarily requires an experienced, talented cast and a highly imaginative director and designers. *The Fantasticks, The Apple Tree, Two by Two, Company,* and *A Chorus Line* are good examples of ensemble shows that are relatively easy to produce if you have the requisite talented cast. *A Chorus Line* without talented actor/singer/dancers would be a disaster.

5. *The musical revue.* A musical revue generally has no plot, no book, a small cast (four performers seems to be average), and lots and lots of music. Shows like *Side by Side by Sondheim* and *Jacques Brel Is Alive and Well and Living in Paris* are extremely attractive to amateur organizations, although they do require talented and personable performers with very good voices. Revues are relatively inexpensive to produce, don't need a big orchestra (four or five musicians, sometimes fewer), and can be done in a relatively short rehearsal period. Revues work best in small theatres of no more than a few hundred seats. The audience comes to a revue to hear the music and to develop a one-on-one relationship with the performers. A large performance space tends to overwhelm the small cast and discourages an intimate relationship between cast and audience.

6. *The operetta.* Not exactly a musical and not exactly an opera, an operetta is an interesting combination of both. The emphasis is on singing, as in an opera, but operettas employ elements of musical theatre, such as acting and dancing, to a much greater degree than do most operas. There is a clear delineation between principals, secondary roles, and chorus, as in an opera, and the music in an operetta is designed primarily to showcase the performer and rarely advances the plot. (Although most operettas have more of a plot to advance than operas do.) Operettas require trained singers with a greater singing range than is generally required in most musicals, and the principal roles in an operetta are usually written for sopranos and tenors rather than mezzo-sopranos and baritones. There tend to be few set or costume changes in an operetta, which considerably simplifies the technical requirements. Operettas are usually period pieces, however, which can be expensive, particularly if period costumes must be rented. One major drawback to an amateur production of an operetta like *Pirates of Penzance* or *The Student Prince* is that excellent singers are necessary in the lead male roles and a large male chorus is also required. (A recurrent problem in amateur theatre companies is the scarcity of talented male singers.)

Operettas are a good choice, however, for theatres affiliated with adult choral groups or school choirs and for such musical organizations on their own.

7. *Combination shows. Camelot* is a book musical with considerable spectacle, as is *The King and I. Fiddler on the Roof, The Music Man,* and *Man of La Mancha* are star vehicles that nevertheless have a good book. *Gypsy,* in addition to being a star vehicle, contains elements of spectacle. *Funny Girl* is a star vehicle with a good book *and* spectacle. All revues are ensemble shows by nature, but not all ensemble shows are revues. *Sophisticated Ladies* is a revue performed by an ensemble. *The Fantasticks* is an ensemble show, although it does share many of the characteristics of a revue— small cast, minimal set and costumes, small orchestra. *The Fantasticks* has a book and an actual plot, as does *Company,* another ensemble show, whereas *Jacques Brel Is Alive and Well and Living in Paris* does not.

Talent Pool ■ There are many more variables associated with casting a musical than with casting a straight play. You must consider the size of the cast, for instance, and the nature, style, and complexity of the music and the choreography. You need to weigh all the performance requirements very carefully in relation to the available talent pool.

A "small" musical like *Dames at Sea* can easily be performed by a cast of seven young actor/singer/dancers, whereas a "big" musical like *The Sound of Music* demands a cast of twenty-four, including seven children, and a large singing and dancing chorus. Speaking of children, *Annie, Oliver!,* and *The King and I* could hardly be performed without them. *George M!* or *Anything Goes* are not good choices if you have no tap-dancers, nor is *Carousel, Kismet, Sweeney Todd, West Side Story,* or *The Most Happy Fella* a good choice if you have only marginally talented singers. *A Little Night Music* requires only five men and eight women, no chorus, and very little dancing, which is well within the range of most amateur organizations, but the cast must be excellent actor/singers, experienced, mature, and able to portray sexually sophisticated characters. *Barnum* requires that the cast not only possess acting, singing, and dancing skills, but also be adept at playing a variety of musical instruments and be capable of performing many *circus* stunts as well, including acrobatics, juggling, tightrope walking, and high-flying on the trapeze! Oddly enough, the chorus of *Barnum,* which performs most of these circus acts as well as doubling many small roles, must be even more multitalented than the principals.

There are many, many musicals currently available for production—from Gilbert and Sullivan to Lerner and Lowe, Stephen Sondheim to Andrew Lloyd Webber—everything from a cast of two, like *I Do! I Do!*, to "a cast of thousands," like *Annie Get Your Gun, Mame,* or *The Music Man.* One of them is very likely tailor-made for your organization.

Resist the sometimes overwhelming temptation to choose a musical that you've always, *always* wanted to direct, hoping that the necessary talent will somehow magically appear at auditions. It probably won't. Also resist choosing a show just to showcase one or two people in your talent pool, no matter how talented (or persuasive) they may be. Evaluate each show as a *total* production package. Available talent is only one part of the picture.

Audience ■ All audiences love musicals, but not all audiences love all musicals. What may be perfectly acceptable in one community—*Cabaret, Sweet Charity,* or *Irma La Douce,* for instance—might be perfectly scandalous in another. A young audience might appreciate *Grease, Bye, Bye Birdie,* or even *You're a Good Man, Charlie Brown,* but an older crowd might prefer *Guys and Dolls, South Pacific,* or *My Fair Lady.* A Stephen Sondheim musical like *Into the Woods* or *Sunday in the Park with George* will appeal to a sophisticated audience, as will *A Little Night Music,* but the same shows may be less well received among a general audience.

Know your customers. With few exceptions, you will be doing the musical *for them.* It's not necessarily a matter of pandering to your audience or of "giving them what they want," but of giving them what you think that they'll consider coming to see. You've got to get them in the door before you can educate them or attempt to alter their perceptions about musicals. If you do a bang-up job of *South Pacific* this year, then maybe next year your audience will be open to something a little different, a little more challenging, and you can present *Pacific Overtures.*

Facilities ■ Questions, questions, questions. Where are you going to put the orchestra? Is there space for multiple, simultaneous rehearsals? Is there more than one piano, or will the same beat-up relic have to be shuttled from one rehearsal room to another on its three wheels and spindly legs? Are there facilities and equipment for building the sets? Is there enough space backstage to store the sets and still have room for the cast and crew? Is there enough dressing room space? Do you have enough lighting instruments, including spotlights, or will additional equipment need to be purchased or rented?

Will you be able to build the costumes in-house, or will they, too, have to be rented? Where will the costumes be stored? Will they be safe? Will the singers be miked (which is increasingly the case in amateur productions)? Will the singers need to perform the show to a taped accompaniment (always problematic)? If so, is good-quality sound equipment available, or will it also have to be rented?

Technical Requirements ■ The scenic and costuming demands a musical places on a producing organization can be daunting. In some instances, however, the rental-catalog descriptions of the set and costume requirements are misleading. It's important that you explore alternative types of staging with your design staff. *Camelot, My Fair Lady,* or *The Sound of Music* might not work too well on a bare stage with minimal costumes, but there are a number of musicals, such as *Company, The Fantasticks, Pippin,* and *A Funny Thing Happened on the Way to the Forum,* that lend themselves quite nicely to simple sets and simple yet effective costuming. Some "larger" shows, like *Damn Yankees, Fiddler on the Roof,* and *Once Upon a Mattress,* are not overly demanding, technically speaking, but *A Little Night Music,* a small-cast show with wonderful music, is set in turn-of-the-century Sweden and requires period costumes and two basic sets, plus projections—all at considerable expense. *Barnum* requires functional circus equipment, and first-rate safety measures need to be taken to ensure the well-being of the cast while performing the circus stunts that are part of the show. *Little Shop of Horrors* requires only two basic and fairly simple sets—a two-room interior and a street scene—but the man-and-woman-eating plant that is the central "character" of the musical requires many hours of preparation and separate rehearsals in which to coordinate the plant's offstage voice with its onstage activities.

Budget ■ Musicals are expensive. Sets, lighting, costumes, other technical production aspects, publicity, and promotion will all cost more, and royalties and rental fees will be one of the largest single budget items, if not the highest production cost overall.

Performance Rights ■ Acquiring the rights to perform a musical is considerably more complex and can be considerably more expensive than acquiring the rights to a straight play. In addition to a considerable royalty fee, you will need to pay in advance for the rental of the scripts, the score, orchestra parts, chorus parts, and anything extra that you may need to rehearse and stage the production.

The minimum rental fee quoted by the rental agency gets you the minimum materials necessary to rehearse and perform the show—a barely adequate number of scripts, dialogue parts ("sides"), scores, vocal/chorus parts, and orchestra parts. Anything else involves an additional fee, often quite substantial.

If you read music, you will probably want to rent an extra score for yourself, as well as extra scores for the choreographer and the rehearsal accompanist. The "sides" (an abbreviated script containing only the actor's cues and lines) included in some rental packages are useless for rehearsing all but the minor roles. You may need to rent additional full scripts. If you have a large number of singers, you may need more choral parts than are supplied in the basic package.

Tell your business manager how much you need (adjusted upward to account for the usual and expected attrition necessitated by "budgetary limitations"), and hope for the best. Unless you have an unlimited budget, you can expect to have to make do with less than the ideal quantity of rehearsal materials.

Musical production rights, particularly for the most popular musicals, are in considerable demand by theatres throughout the country (and throughout the world, for that matter). For example, the first year *My Fair Lady* was available to amateur organizations there were more than *ten thousand* productions. The Rodgers and Hammerstein Library, which acts as the agent for the Rodgers and Hammerstein estate, licensed over seven hundred productions of *Oklahoma!* in 1993, the musical's fiftieth anniversary year. *Flower Drum Song,* a moderately popular Rodgers and Hammerstein musical that requires a predominantly Asian American cast, is produced one hundred times a year. Even lesser-known R & H musicals like *Pipe Dream* and *Me and Juliet* average one or two productions a month, most of them in university theatres.

Rental agencies know there is a strong possibility that you are going to make money with one of their musicals, so they charge a proportionate fee for the performance rights and rental materials. Your ticket prices can probably be raised accordingly, not only because of the higher cost of a producing a musical, but also in anticipation of an increased demand for tickets. Musicals are popular attractions, and people are willing to pay a premium to attend.

The royalties that the rental agency will quote for your production will be based on (1) your ticket prices, (2) the capacity of your theatre or auditorium, (3) the number of performances, and (4) whether or not you require an orchestration. With these considerations in mind, ask yourself if there are enough seats in the theatre to make the production of a particular musical economically feasible. In other words, will five hundred seats at ten dollars a seat for ten nights pay for this show? What if the house is only half full? (Note that one of the criteria for your royalty quotation is the *capacity* of the theatre, *not* the number of tickets sold. *You* assume the risk of not filling those seats, not the rental agency.) There is also a *minimum* royalty fee, although it's not advertised as such, no matter how small your theatre may be, so what do you do if there are only fifty seats in your theatre? Will it still be feasible to stage this show if you have to charge Broadway ticket prices? (Maybe it's time to think about doing a revue instead.)

All the costs associated with a musical are directly related to all the other costs. The longer you run the show, the more the royalties will cost. The more the royalties cost, the more tickets you have to sell, at a higher price. The more tickets you want to sell, the more you have to advertise. The more you advertise, the higher the advertising costs . . . and so on. In time, you will reach a point of diminishing returns—the show will cost much more than it's worth to your organization to produce. You need to balance the popularity of the show (potential ticket sales) with the cost of the show (royalties, set, costumes, advertising, and so on), and consider all other pertinent factors (ticket prices and projected attendance) in arriving at a reasonable and monetarily feasible choice.

If you have a substantial budget for the show, by all means spend it. If, however, your production budget is like so many others, you will have to do the best you can with limited funds. Even then, however, a show can still look good and sound good. Spend money where the audience can see it and hear it—on the costumes, set, orchestra, and sound system. Decide on your priorities, as you would for a straight play. Remember, though, that an audience that doesn't mind Shakespeare's *Taming of the Shrew* done in modern dress on a bare stage expects more, *much* more, from a production of *Kiss Me, Kate.*

For a musical on a limited budget, it's all a matter of priorities and compromise. Generally speaking, put money into costumes first. Great costumes, even on a simple set, act as moving scenery, and highlight the performers. The cost of the costumes will vary greatly, of course, depending on the size of the cast and the historical period in which the musical takes place. The question that next arises is, Are you going to build the costumes in-house or are you going to rent them? If you build them, you will need to hire a costume designer and an experienced costume construction crew. If you rent them, you need hire only a costumer—someone to supervise the use and care of the rented costumes—and a few costuming assistants (or use volunteers from the cast). Costume designers are more expensive than costumers. If you hire a costume designer, you may have to hire a costumer as well. If you rent the costumes, you can put the difference in salary between a costume designer (and costume construction crew) and a costumer (and assistants) into the rental budget instead. Work out the math both ways to determine what's most cost efficient.

There are two elements to consider relative to the *sound* of the show—the sound system and the orchestra. On the one hand, nothing compares with the sound of a full orchestra launching headlong into the overture and providing a lush setting for the singers. On the other hand, nothing compares with being unable to *hear* the singers because the orchestra is too loud, the sound system is poor, or the theatre is too large or is acoustically ill suited to musical productions.

This matter of priorities and compromise is an interesting dilemma that theatre organizations face every day. Bottom line: the performers must be seen, and they must be heard. Once those criteria are met, you can parcel out the remaining few dollars in any way that you believe will best serve the production.

STAFFING

The organizational chart for a musical production in Figure 5–1 is essentially identical to the organizational chart for a play in Figure 1–1 (page 16), with some added staff members. The additional staff for a musical may include an assistant stage manager, assistant director, music director/conductor, rehearsal accompanist, musicians, and a choreographer. You may need additional technical people as well, particularly for set and costume construction and backstage running crews. Consult your technical advisers and expand your technical support staff accordingly.

Assistant Stage Manager ■ This position already appears on the standard organizational chart, but some organizations choose to do without an assistant stage manager, particularly for small productions. For a musical, however, an ASM is needed to take some of the load off the stage manager, who will be very busy. The ASM can act as a liaison between and among simultaneous rehearsals for actors, dancers, and singers, and between the stage manager and technical staff, particularly during dress rehearsal week. The ASM might also serve as prompter (in a play *or* musical), thereby relieving the stage manager of that responsibility.

Assistant Director ■ Some directors like to go it alone. It is advisable, however, *not* to go it alone in a musical. The AD can be where you can't. He can supervise rehearsals when you have to be

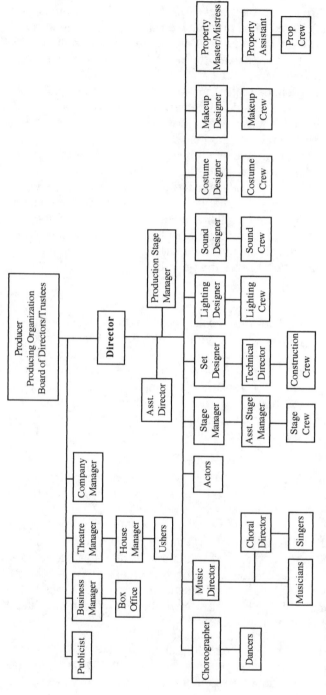

Figure 5–1. Theatre Organization Chart for a Musical

elsewhere—at a dance or vocal rehearsal, for instance, or in a meeting with design or technical personnel. The AD can take notes for you, relieving the stage manager of yet another responsibility, and he can supervise small-group rehearsals while you attend to the big picture.

Music Director/Conductor ■ The music director is responsible for all things musical—for every note that is sung or played. He prepares the musical score for the production, rehearses the singers, organizes and rehearses the orchestra, and may also conduct the orchestra for performances. An average musical contains fifteen or more musical numbers, an overture, entr'acte, and other not-so-incidental music, all of it the music director's responsibility.

The music director should be someone who knows and understands the musical theatre production process (as well as a nontheatre person can be expected to understand it). He should also be experienced in his field, able to engage a good rehearsal accompanist, and to recruit a decent orchestra (also his responsibility), preferably from among his friends and colleagues.

If it is the custom in your organization for the director to hire the music director, you should begin to cultivate friendships in the music world early in your career. Last-minute personnel choices, particularly when you need to find someone *fast,* rarely work out well. The most effective music director will be one who has been part of the production team very early on.

If you are a novice director, try to work with the most experienced music director you can find. His experience and advice will be invaluable. You may find, however, that as a novice director you may well be working with a novice music director. This is not all that unfortunate. It will give both of you a chance to learn, together, the intricacies of mounting a musical. You may also develop a good working relationship that will serve you well over the years.

Rehearsal Accompanist ■ One of the most important decisions the music director will make (and one you should be aware of) is choosing a rehearsal accompanist. The rehearsal accompanist must be dedicated, above all. This uniquely talented person must be willing to be on call for long hours of rehearsal over an extended period. He must be supremely confident and competent, unselfish, with a pleasant disposition—not given to panic, fits of pique, or displays of "artistic temperament"—and possess an extraordinary sense of humor. He's going to need it.

Occasionally, particularly in small amateur organizations, the music director, the rehearsal accompanist, and the conductor may be the same person. There doesn't seem to be any particular advantage or disadvantage to this situation, other than that the person will be seriously overworked. Unless the orchestra is very small, however, the music director should not conduct the orchestra from the piano. Encourage him to engage another pianist for the performances.

Musicians ■ The musicians for the production will be chosen by the music director. A standard orchestra for a musical production comprises sixteen to twenty musicians. Unless the music is scored for a small group, encourage the music director to engage as large an orchestra as the budget will allow. There is nothing like the sound of a full (and well-rehearsed) orchestra launching into the overture. The effect on the audience is immediate and magical. Once the cast hears those first few familiar notes of the overture, you won't have any problem getting them up for the show.

A large orchestra may cause some problems for the singers, however, particularly if the singers are not miked. Suggest that the music director cut back on the size of the orchestra during parts of the vocal numbers to allow the singers to be heard. If the singers are miked, a large orchestra shouldn't be a problem.

Choreographer ■ The choreographer is responsible for devising and staging the dance numbers, rehearsing the dancers, and (if this is agreeable to the director) supervising all dance-associated movement onstage.

The choreographer will likely choose one of his dancers to serve as an assistant choreographer or dance captain. This person will assist the choreographer by rehearsing small groups of dancers, helping stage vocal numbers involving dance sequences, and so on.

The choreographer will also need the rehearsal accompanist, or someone equally familiar with the musical score, to play for the dance rehearsals. It is possible to use tape-recorded accompaniment for the dance rehearsals, however. Many choreographers are experienced in working this way, and although turning the tape recorder on and off and forwarding and rewinding the tape does slow down the rehearsal a little, it is certainly better than having no accompaniment at all. Since the music director or rehearsal accompanist has probably already recorded the dance music for the choreographer's use in working up the staging of the dance numbers, it should be a simple transition to use the tape recording in rehearsal as well.

There will be times, of course, when only a real, live accompanist will do, particularly in the early stages of rehearsals and again near the end and possibly as each dance number is completed. Expect to lose your regular rehearsal accompanist to the choreographer every now and again. If you rehearse acting sequences during his absence, the impact on your rehearsals will be minimal.

Make sure you and the choreographer understand your individual areas of responsibility regarding each musical number. Generally speaking, you are responsible for the overall staging of the show and of the movement (not the dancing) of the principals within the musical numbers. The choreographer is responsible for the interior staging of musical numbers—the movement and dancing of the vocal chorus and dancers and the dancing of the principals—and the overall staging of dance numbers.

The choreographer may also sometimes be responsible for the movement of the principals within the musical numbers. In a professional working relationship, the good of the production will be the focus of the director's and choreographer's efforts. Staging tasks very likely will be shared. The director may ask the choreographer to help stage transitions between acting and dancing, for instance, or to take over the staging of an entire musical number, chorus and principals alike.

The music director and choreographer, as well as other members of your artistic staff, may have been assigned before you arrived on the scene. If so, meet with these people as soon as possible, and confer with them on the overall production, the auditions, and the rehearsal schedule. If you get to know them early enough in the process, you can also ask their advice about which musical to do. They may also be familiar with the available talent and with local music and dance resources, all of which will make your life considerably easier.

Casting

Again we've come to that moment of truth—casting the show. All that has gone before will mean little if the production falls short in the casting. Review the auditioning and casting guidelines in Chapter 2. Much of what applies to casting a play also applies to casting a musical.

PREAUDITION PREPARATION

Before the auditions, get together with your music director and choreographer and decide on your evaluation criteria, as you would for a straight play. Be sure, first, that you're all speaking the same language. The music director and choreographer know quite well what they mean by certain words and phrases they use, but you may not. Likewise, they may not completely understand what you're saying to them.

"Moves well," for instance, does not necessarily mean the same as "can dance." "Can sing" does not mean ". . . at home, alone, in the shower." "Can act" does not mean "can read aloud words of less than three syllables." Define your terms for one another. It will help avoid misunderstandings during the casting process and will save considerable time during all your discussions during rehearsals.

The director, the music director, and the choreographer should serve as the casting committee. In case of any dispute or disagreement over casting, the director should have the deciding vote. Don't divide the casting decisions, letting the director cast the principals and straight acting roles, the music director cast the singing roles and the chorus, and the choreographer cast all the dancers. This invariably leads to disputes about multitalented actors. Work together for the best possible *combination* of actors, singers, and dancers for the production.

Sometimes the casting is done by a casting committee from the producing organization, who may or may not possess the necessary skills to evaluate the talent before them. Casting by committee can be highly subjective—particularly when friends and/or relatives are involved—disorganized, time-consuming, contentious, and potentially disastrous.

Casting politics is a touchy subject, but the artistic staff really should be able to cast their own show. If you find your casting subject to the approval of a committee, or if casting is taken out of your hands altogether, ask yourself whether you really want this job.

When you're sure that you, the music director, and the choreographer are all speaking the same language, discuss the essential, *ideal* requirements for each role in terms of acting, singing, and/or dancing. Also decide on the *minimum* level of skills and abilities required, or that each of you will accept. By having a clear idea of what you are looking for in auditions, *in advance,* you will avoid unnecessary misunderstandings and disagreements.

You may decide among you, for instance, that the ideal performer you choose for the role of, say, Henry Higgins in *My Fair Lady* or King Arthur in *Camelot* or the King in *The King And I* should be a good actor, a fair singer, and a fair dancer. The minimum requirements for the roles require only that the performer be a good actor with a decent musical sense; he needn't be able to sing or dance well at all. Ideally, the performer you choose for the role of Eliza in *My Fair*

Lady or Guenevere in *Camelot* or Fanny Brice in *Funny Girl* or Anna in *The King And I* should be an excellent singer, a good actress, and a fair dancer. The minimum qualifications for these roles are that the performer be an excellent singer and a decent, competent actress. Naturally you will want to cast the ideal performer in each role, but the person you cast will most likely fall somewhere between your minimum and ideal expectations.

Determine what you will be looking for in terms of casting the singing and/or dancing *chorus* as well. Acting talent is not required, of course, but singing and dancing skills should be fairly decent. Do take the time and make the necessary effort to cast the members of the chorus as carefully as you cast the rest of the show. Consider each person for individual talents as well as for contributions to the production as a whole.

Also give some thought to the bit parts, walk-ons, and extras. To some extent, the casting of these incidental roles can be decided in rehearsal and will be determined by which performers are available at that point in the show. Still, you should have some idea of the relative skills of each available performer relative to the available roles. Singing roles require singers, dancing roles require dancers, and character roles require actors. Casting these roles should not be haphazard or arbitrary.

It may be the tradition in your organization to simply put everyone who auditions but who is not cast in a real role into the chorus. Even so, you and the music director and choreographer still need some idea of their skills in order to assign the small roles that "the gentlemen and ladies of the chorus" are expected to fill.

Next, decide among yourselves how the auditions will be run. You need to schedule either simultaneous or sequential acting, vocal, and dance auditions, so that each of you will have a chance to evaluate each auditioner. If you expect a large turnout, it is preferable to schedule the auditions over two or three days—acting auditions one day, singing and dance auditions the next, or any other combination. A sign-up list for the acting and singing auditions will help ease the burden on the staff *and* the auditioners. Part of the dance auditions will probably be conducted *en masse,* particularly the first general audition, so set aside some time for that, as well as for individual or small-group follow-ups or callbacks.

As for audition material, you, the director, will choose the acting sequences, the music director will likely choose from the musical numbers in the show (or the auditioner will sing a prepared musical selection), and the choreographer will devise his own dance/movement audition.

AUDITIONS

If you believe the auditions can be managed in just one day, schedule them simultaneously—acting in one room, singing in another, and dancing in yet another, possibly on the stage. Divide the auditioners into manageable groups, and shuttle them (and their audition forms) from one activity to another with the help of your stage manager and other assistants. Allow sufficient time in each audition for a fair evaluation of each person, but try to adhere to your schedule as best you can. It's sometimes a grueling experience for auditioners and staff alike, but unless you have the luxury of an extended period of time at your disposal, it's best to consolidate the auditions into one massive effort.

It may be possible, with a smallish, more manageable turnout, to schedule the auditions sequentially. Start, for example, with the singing auditions. Allow the music director some time to do vocal warm-ups with the entire group, then let him proceed with the vocal auditions. Move the group to the dance auditions. Again, allow the choreographer time to warm up the auditioners. Following the dance auditions, move everyone to the acting auditions.

There are several advantages to this sequential audition schedule. First, it allows the director, music director, and choreographer an opportunity to view all the auditioners in all three areas, thereby allowing them to form a more complete evaluation. Second, it allows the auditioners time to warm up and to prepare themselves mentally and physically for each type of audition. Finally, it also gives the auditioners an opportunity to see all the other auditioners in action.

In your preaudition announcements, tell potential auditioners *all* the particulars. Include not only time and place, but also a description of the major roles, precasting (if any), types and length of prepared readings or songs required, whether or not an accompanist will be provided, dates of performance, and anything else that will help each auditioner prepare.

CALLBACKS

The sequential arrangement described above also works well for callbacks. First, get together with your music director and choreographer and decide on which actors to call back. (It is not necessary to call back those on whose casting you already agree. Use callbacks only to make decisions about roles that are undecided.) Then have your stage manager prepare and post the callback list.

At the callback, give a short explanation of the procedure and get to it. Take as much time as you need (within reason) to evaluate each actor. Most of the actors who make it this far will be in no hurry to leave. They want to make sure you have a good look at them, and you want to be sure they are given ample opportunity to show their stuff.

CASTING CONSIDERATIONS

You can expect that your music director will lobby for the best singers, of course, and that your choreographer will want the best dancers. If it were only that simple.

Begin the casting process by listing those performers who possess the minimum qualifications for each role. In some cases, there may be only one person who meets even the minimum criteria for a particular role. In that case, immediately cast that performer in that role, even though he may be suitable for other roles, and cross his name off all other lists. Resist the temptation to hold out for better roles for one or more of your auditioners. If he is the only person who fulfills the requirements for a role, cast him and be done with it.

You may find that by casting the one-candidate-only roles, you have shortened a few remaining lists to only one person. Cast those people as well. By casting those roles for which there is only one choice *first,* you will save a considerable amount of time and you will avoid second-guessing yourself (and each other) about every role.

Next, cast the remaining major roles, secondary roles, and minor roles, in that order. Evaluate each list of names to find the performer who is most *ideally* suited to each role. If you find one, cast him in that role and cross him off all other lists. Again, you may find that doing so simplifies casting of another role.

More often than not, however, there will be no one who perfectly fits the criteria for some roles. In this case, you return to your list of priorities. You may be casting Henry Higgins in *My Fair Lady,* for example, and you have two casting choices. One is a good actor, a passable singer, and a poor dancer. The other is a good actor, a poor singer, but a good dancer. Who will you cast? Your priorities were acting first, singing second, and dancing last. Cast the actor/singer and cross him off the other lists. Repeat the process until you have cast all the principal, secondary, and minor roles in the show.

Talented performers occasionally lose out in this type of casting. Console yourself with the knowledge that you have cast the best person for each role, in the best interests of the production.

If you and your music director and/or choreographer disagree about casting or if you are torn between equally talented performers, you, the director, must decide. If you are a novice director, don't be intimidated by a more experienced music director or choreographer.

Listen to their advice, rely on their expertise, but don't abdicate your responsibility for casting the production to them or to anyone else. You are the artistic head of the production. You are ultimately responsible for *everything* related to the artistic fulfillment of every element and of every person connected with it. It's *your* show. Expect that your music director and choreographer will abide by your decision, and that they'll be professional about it.

In spite of your best efforts and the well-intentioned advice of your colleagues, you may find yourself unable to decide which of two or three performers should get a particular role. All is not lost. You needn't resort to drawing names out of a hat or throwing darts at résumés on the wall. Figure 5–2 is a general casting guide that assumes a performer is primarily an actor, a singer, or a dancer, with additional skills in one or two other areas and suggests logical, conservative casting choices based on these relative strengths. You can adapt the guide to your own priorities and casting criteria.

Obviously, the more skills someone possesses, the greater the casting opportunities. Just because an actor can't sing, however, or sings poorly, is no reason not to cast the performer in a musical. There are a number of nonsinging, nondancing roles, particularly character roles, in many musicals, particularly those with a large cast. Rather than cast a mediocre actor who can also sing or dance in such a part, cast the straight actor instead. Cast the actor/singer/dancer in another role, or in the chorus, and rely on the straight actor to bring out the best he has to offer in the character role.

Think hard before casting a singer in a major role solely for his or her voice. The temptation is to cast the voice, not the person, and hope that you can somehow teach the singer to act and dance in time for opening night. Sometimes this strategy works. More often than not, however, the singer never learns to act *or* dance, and stands there like a stick through the whole show, or acts and dances so poorly that it's embarrassing. Cast the *overall* best person for each role, according to your predetermined criteria.

Dancing singers and singing dancers seem to be somewhat shortchanged as to casting opportunities. It's unfortunate, but singers and dancers who can't act are at a distinct disadvantage. Acting is a basic, essential skill for any theatrical performer. Encourage dancers and singers who hope to be musical theatre performers to take acting classes to improve their skills. Those who are serious about their career will take your advice. The rest will probably remain in the chorus.

As when casting a play, cast talent over type. Choose more experienced over less experienced, real age over age makeup, and

Skill(s)	*Casting*
Actors who can sing and dance.	Lead or secondary roles in singing/acting/dancing musicals.
Actors who can sing.	Lead or secondary nondancing roles, singing character roles.
Actors who can dance.	Secondary, nonsinging roles, character roles.
Actors, period.	Straight acting roles, character roles, nonsinging secondary or minor roles, walk-ons, bit parts.
Singers who can act and dance.	Lead or secondary roles in singing/acting/dancing musicals.
Singers who can act.	Lead or secondary nondancing roles, singing character roles.
Singers who can dance.	Chorus.
Singers, period.	Nondancing chorus.
Dancers who can act and sing.	Lead or secondary roles in dancing musicals. Secondary roles in singing/acting musicals.
Dancers who can sing.	Dancing chorus.
Dancers who can act.	Dancing chorus, nonsinging character roles, nonsinging secondary roles, walk-ons, bit parts.
Dancers, period.	Dancing chorus, featured dancer.

Figure 5–2. A Generic Musical Casting Guide

younger to play older (rather than older to play younger). Choose those who are easily directed over those who seem to have a problem taking your suggestions. Choose intelligence, ability, personality, and imagination.

Double-casting (often done in school productions and occasionally in other amateur productions) serves only one useful (if highly doubtful) purpose: it relieves the director of the responsibility of making a difficult casting decision. Rarely are performers equally matched in *all* their talents. Rarely will they perform equally well onstage. And rarely will the director have the time necessary to rehearse both performers (or both casts) to an equally high performance level. What seems extremely fair at first—giving two performers a chance to perform in the same role—is in fact a disservice, not only to the performers, but to the production. The director cannot abdicate his responsibility to the production. He must simply bite the bullet and decide which performer gets the role.

Remember the old adage that casting accounts for 90 percent of the ultimate success (or failure) of a production. In the case of a musical, that estimate may be somewhat conservative.

ALTERNATES AND UNDERSTUDIES

After you've completed your casting process, go through the entire list of names again and decide on an alternate choice for each principal and secondary role. Choose most if not all of these alternates from the chorus and those in minor roles. Otherwise, you will be playing musical chairs with the leading performers if one of them has to leave the show.

An alternate is not the same as an understudy. An alternate is an alternate *casting* choice, should the first choice refuse the assigned role or drop out of the show (or be invited to leave) at some later date. Unlike an understudy, the alternate is not announced. The director, music director, and choreographer know who the alternates are, but there is no need to make the alternates known to the cast (or to the alternates, for that matter) unless the alternate must take over the role.

The major drawback to assigning understudies is that understudies must be rehearsed. For the most part, understudies are unnecessary in a musical because everybody learns everybody else's lines, songs, and blocking anyway. This is particularly true in amateur productions. Almost anyone in the chorus could (and would probably love to, die to, kill to) take over a secondary or leading role on a moment's notice.

Except in a long-running professional production, understudies almost never have to go on. The odds of an *alternate* taking over a role are much greater. Because of the large number of people in the cast of most musicals and the length of the rehearsal period, it is a very good bet that someone will leave the show before it opens. A major role can be taken over by an actor in a minor role, and the minor role taken over by someone in the chorus—even at the last minute before curtain on opening night.

Preparing the Script

The contract that your organization is required to sign in order to produce the musical usually includes a stipulation that no changes may be made to the script or to the music without the written consent of the author(s) or the agency from whom you acquired the rights to the show. If you intend to cut any of the dialogue or musical numbers, you will need that consent. You are not likely to get it.

Some directors choose to ignore the "no changes" provision of their production contract and cut the show to suit their purposes. They see no harm in cutting a line or two (or more), rearranging the order of songs, or cutting a dance sequence out of a musical number. Of course this destroys the integrity of the show, but since it is a violation of the contract, it can have serious (and potentially very costly) consequences for the producing organization. As the director, it is your responsibility to maintain the integrity of the production in *all* aspects, including the integrity of the words and music. Rather than risk the financial ruin of your organization (not to mention your own professional ruin), either do the musical as written or find another show that's more to your liking.

On a related subject, rented materials supplied for most musicals generally contain discrepancies between the lyrics in the piano/conductor score and in the vocal parts, which may also be different from the lyrics in the printed script. It's a simple matter to reconcile these differences: choose the word that's easier to sing. If one word isn't appreciably easier to sing than another, take a vote among the artistic staff and let the majority rule, or make the decision yourself. You might get an argument from the author or the lyricist (or the typist) about your final choice, but you will not be in violation of your production contract by resolving these minor discrepancies. The only concern here is the time that will be wasted discussing these discrepancies in rehearsal if the matter is not resolved in advance.

Production Meetings

Production meetings should be scheduled regularly throughout the production process. Except for the general meeting regarding the master rehearsal schedule (see page 134), it is best to conduct two different sets of production meetings—one for you and the design and technical personnel and another for yourself, the music director, and the choreographer. There is little reason for all these people to meet together as a "committee of the whole."

It is true that the choreographer needs to know about the placement of the set and furniture and overall stage spacing. For the most part, however, this information can be conveyed by the director or the stage manager. The choreographer may also wish to use furniture or other props in his dance rehearsals. The show furniture and show props will probably not be available for rehearsals until very near the end of the rehearsal period, possibly not until dress rehearsals. Adequate, functional substitutes will have to be found, a responsibility best left to a resourceful stage manager and props person.

The *design production meetings* should function in much the same way as they do when you are directing a straight play. You can expect significantly more technical problems in a musical than in a straight play, and these problems will be bigger. There's just so much more to go wrong, and in a much bigger way. Even minor problems can affect many people, in many areas of production. Schedule design and technical meetings more frequently than for a straight play. If there aren't any problems, cancel the meeting. If problems do arise (as they will), they won't have gone unrecognized or unresolved for very long. Also, make sure any department head knows he can call a meeting with you or other relevant personnel at any time to address and resolve a pressing problem.

The (for want of a better term) *artistic production meetings*—involving you, the music director, and the choreographer—should include status reports on the progress of each aspect of rehearsals—acting, music, and dance. This is the time to explore options regarding the challenges and problems that arise during the rehearsals. A consensus is not necessary, of course, but unilateral decisions by the director without the knowledge, advice, and/or and consent of the music director and/or choreographer are not recommended. Unilateral decisions will increasingly alienate the music director and/or choreographer and may seriously undermine the effectiveness of your working relationship. A strained relationship, even among professionals, will ultimately affect the quality of the production.

Schedule production meetings with your music director and choreographer at regular intervals, daily if necessary. This way you will be able to adjust the rehearsal schedule to accommodate any additional rehearsals for music or dance or otherwise fine tune the schedule as you go along, depending on how things are progressing overall.

Master Schedule

The master production schedule contains the date, time, and place of every rehearsal and all relevant deadlines (including design and technical deadlines), from the initial planning for the show through the postproduction evaluation. This schedule will not be distributed to the cast, who are concerned only with their own acting, music, and dance rehearsals. The master schedule is for the benefit of the heads of the artistic and design departments, for the producing organization, and for the management of the theatre.

The master schedule for a musical should include many, if not all, of the following deadlines:

- Ordering of rental materials for cast and orchestra
- Expected receipt of ordered rental materials
- Audition announcements
- Production meetings—artistic and design
- Auditions
- Rehearsal dates, times, and places
- Orchestra rehearsals (without cast)
- Construction deadlines for set, props, costumes
- Ordering deadline for rented costumes
- Expected arrival of rented costumes
- Publicity and photo sessions (Provided by the front office.)
- Social functions involving artistic or design staff or cast members (Also provided by the front office.)
- Deadlines for technical elements of production—set, lights, sound
- Technical move-in dates (if theatre is rented or unavailable until late in the rehearsal period)
- Backstage crew meetings
- Technical and dress rehearsals
- Performances
- Postproduction evaluation meetings

Other deadlines relevant to your particular theatre organization should be included on the master schedule, as appropriate.

Naturally you will work with the heads of each department in developing the master schedule. Hold a meeting with as many representatives of each department as are available—designers, crew heads, technical director, front-office and publicity representatives, and so on, plus the stage manager, whose responsibility it is to mediate disputes and to sooth bruised egos. It is important that every department be represented at this meeting to avoid conflicts and disagreements over deadlines and expectations that may arise later. Tell those who are reluctant to attend (or who may be just "too busy") that they need to appoint someone to represent their interests at the meeting; if the schedule is drawn up without them, they can't complain if it doesn't suit them.

After the master schedule has been approved, the director, music director, and choreographer need to schedule rehearsals for each artistic element of the production. Sequester yourselves with the stage manager, and get to work. Don't leave the room until a tentative schedule of all rehearsals is complete and agreeable to all.

After casting is completed, get together again with your artistic staff to fine-tune the schedule to accommodate performer conflicts, if any, and any other last-minute considerations. Make no accommodations for performers during the final week before opening night, however. If a performer can't be at dress rehearsal, that person should not be in the show. How can you expect to bring all the elements of the show together if some of those elements are missing?

Rehearsal Time Lines

Each element of the musical—acting, music, and dance—will rehearse separately throughout most of the rehearsal period, most particularly during the first few weeks. The principals and chorus will learn their lines and blocking separate from their songs and dances. The musical numbers won't be fully staged until everyone has learned the music and the choreography. Finally, the orchestra will begin rehearsing late in the rehearsal period and will be added to the mix seemingly at the last minute.

REHEARSAL SCHEDULE

Essentially, the rehearsals for a musical move along five separate paths:

1. Learning lines (blocking), music, and choreography.
2. Integrating musical numbers and dance sequences into acting scenes.
3. Putting completed scenes into sequence.
4. Integrating technical elements into completed parts of the show.
5. Integrating the orchestra into the production.

For example, only after Scenes 1 and 2 have been blocked, and the music and dance integrated into the scenes, can the scenes be put in sequence. Only when the majority of the scenes have been put in sequence can the technical elements be integrated. You will follow this progression with different parts of the show simultaneously, of course, but any attempt to short-circuit this process will seriously inhibit the show's development and you will lose valuable rehearsal time. An orderly progression, although not particularly creative, is most effective.

One notable distinction between rehearsing a play and rehearsing a musical is that most of the learning of a musical takes place in the rehearsal hall. The choreography is taught in rehearsal by rote, one step at a time. Those who read music can teach themselves the songs outside of rehearsal, of course, but some members of the cast will not be able to read music, and many will have no place to practice. Learning how the music and choreography fit together is another process, as is the merging of all the elements of acting, music, and dance. These are not things the cast can learn on their own, at home. All of this learning takes place in rehearsal. About the only thing the cast can learn on their own is their lines.

Introduce musical numbers into the blocking and working rehearsals as soon as the actors are minimally competent with the singing and dancing. When preparing the rehearsal schedule, determine tentative deadlines for the musical numbers, and integrate the music and dance into the production as soon as possible thereafter. Adding the musical numbers will slow down the rehearsals at first, but the dividends are great. The musical numbers will gradually become fully integrated into the show, and the show will flow smoothly and seamlessly. The production will be much more unified overall, and the pace will be greatly enhanced.

The director, music director, and choreographer must be present at *all* rehearsals in which acting, music, and choreography are brought together. The director is in charge of these rehearsals. Certainly you should consult the music director and choreographer on anything related to music or choreography, but the ultimate staging decisions are yours. It's your concept, your vision, your show, and your responsibility.

Novice directors are often prone to having frequent full-scale run-throughs. At the first opportunity, the director calls everyone together for a "little run-through," so he "can see how things are shaping up," or "to get some idea of where we are." These periodic run-throughs serve no real purpose other than temporarily to relieve the director's anxiety and insecurities; they waste time better used in enriching and polishing the production. A run-through at the completion of the music, dance, and blocking for each act ought to be sufficient.

It is important that technical and dress rehearsals be scheduled consecutively and that dress rehearsals continue right through to opening night, without a break. Continuity is extremely important, not only within the show, but also from rehearsal to rehearsal. Give your cast every opportunity to do well and to feel confident and secure.

Another important thing to remember when devising your rehearsal schedule, particularly when you're dealing with inexperienced performers, is to arrange the schedule so that the cast never has to face more than one new element of the production at a time. In other words, avoid scheduling makeup *and* costumes, or props *and* set, or any other combination, for the first time at the same rehearsal. Add each new element to the production as soon as it is available and as soon as it is practical, but add only *one* new element at a time. Plan ahead to avoid the twelve-hour, throw-it-*all*-together, technical-plus-orchestra-plus-makeup-and-costume-plus-dress-rehearsal marathon that often seems the staple of amateur theatre organizations.

The *content* of the individual rehearsals is the responsibility of the director, music director, and choreographer, respectively. As the director, you *do* need to monitor progress in each of the areas. Drop in on music and dance rehearsals, as your schedule allows, to see how things are going. Do not disturb or otherwise disrupt the rehearsal. Slip in and out as unobtrusively as possible. Stay only a few minutes. Smile and nod approvingly, and give a thumbs up on your way out. Unless what you observe is total chaos, you can assume that things are proceeding on schedule. If what you observe *is* total chaos, arrange to meet with the appropriate people as soon as possible to effect any necessary changes. Under no circumstances, however, disrupt the rehearsal.

Occasionally, you may be officially invited by the music director or choreographer to attend a rehearsal to view a work in progress or a finished number. Be a considerate guest. Don't make derogatory remarks or negative comments about the work in front of the cast, even if the number is a disaster. You don't want to demoralize or discourage the cast. Take the matter up with the music director or choreographer at another time, in another place. If you are pressed for on-the-spot comments and can find absolutely nothing good to say about what you've seen or heard, say something politically expedient and noncommittal: *The number is really coming along,* or *I can see you've been working very hard on this number, and your work is really starting to pay off,* or *I'm looking forward to seeing the finished number on stage. Keep up the good work.* Smile, nod, thumbs up, and out the door. Then call a meeting and sort things out.

Encourage the music director and choreographer to attend *your* rehearsals and to attend each other's rehearsals, to get a sense of the overall development of the show. Too often the director, music director, and choreographer become isolated in their own rehearsal worlds and fail to develop a sense of the production as a whole.

READ-THROUGH

Follow the general procedure from Chapter 3 for the first reading of a play. Start at the top of the show, and read through to the end, with a short intermission at the act break(s). The stage manager (or some other "designated reader") should read any lines that are unassigned. The principals may sing their songs, if they know them, when they appear in the show, with the chorus members following along as best they can. If the principals don't yet know their songs, the director or music director (or even the choreographer, for that matter), can warble through a verse or two, just to give everyone a rough idea of what the musical numbers sound like in the context of the show.

When the reading is finished, have the stage manager remind the cast of upcoming rehearsals, costume appointments, and any other important information. Some directors like to proceed directly to same-day rehearsals, following a break for lunch or dinner. This will have been determined in advance in the preproduction meetings, and the cast will have been so advised.

VOCAL REHEARSALS

The purpose of vocal rehearsals is to learn the music for the show. In the educational theatre, this may also be an opportunity for the music director to instruct the cast on good vocal production techniques— breathing, tone production, articulation, and so on.

A welcome by-product of vocal rehearsals, one that you may not realize, is the strong sense of ensemble that develops during the course of learning the music for a show. You may find that the chorus for a musical often has a greater sense of camaraderie than do the principals. This stems in part from the onstage hierarchy in a musical and the nature of the rehearsal process—principals rehearse separately from the chorus (and often separately from each other) and are brought together only in the final stages of preparing a scene.

There's little you can do about this, since there's not enough time in the rehearsal schedule for what absolutely *has* to be done, let alone for little camaraderie-building get-togethers for the principals and chorus. If you do find an opportunity to bring your entire cast together, by all means do it. You can only enrich the production by encouraging a sense of ensemble among all the cast members.

DANCE REHEARSALS

Your cast will work very hard in dance rehearsals. Learning the dances is arduous, exhausting, and time-consuming. Dance rehearsals will very likely follow this general procedure: The choreographer or his assistant demonstrates a short sequence of dance steps. This sequence is repeated as many times as necessary until the dancers arrive at a minimal level of competence. Then the sequence is refined and polished. This accomplished, the choreographer moves on to the next step or sequence, following the same procedure until the entire dance has been choreographed. Once the dance number has been learned, the choreographer fine-tunes the dance, adding a touch here, changing a step there, until he is satisfied with the number. The less experienced the dancers are, the longer this process is likely to take. This same one-step-at-a-time process is repeated for every dance number in the show.

Be patient with your choreographer. His job is very demanding. You will find, for the most part, that choreographers are well attuned to the demands of the production schedule and well aware of their own responsibilities and the responsibilities of others within the theatre production process. A competent choreographer will adjust the dances as he goes along to accommodate the learning ability and skills of the dancers. He will simplify difficult steps, for example, or schedule extra rehearsals (within the constraints and demands of the production schedule, of course) to give the dancers ample time to learn the dances.

ORCHESTRA REHEARSALS

Have the music director introduce you at the first orchestra-only rehearsal. Welcome the musicians, express your confidence in them and in the music director, and leave. These people have work to do, and your presence will be disruptive. Yes, you *are* the director of the production, and in many ways you *do* have a right to be there, but you are essentially out of your realm. Even directors who have a strong music background are advised to make themselves scarce during orchestra rehearsals.

Don't hang around to "listen in." If you *do* hang around, you will only get upset. First, the orchestra will not sound very good, particularly in the first few rehearsals. It may seem that the music director spends more time explaining things—cues, tempos, corrections, cuts (and other things you may not understand)—than actually playing the music. You're right. You may think a whole lot of time is being wasted with this kind of talk. It's not. You will see orchestra members coming and going, seemingly at will. If you attend more than one rehearsal, you may see some musicians that you've never seen before, and you will also notice that others are absent.

Does the music director seem concerned about any of these things that upset you so much? Probably not. Despite appearances, he has things well under control. Trust your music director, and trust your musicians. They have as much pride in their work as you have in yours. They didn't sign on for this production just to make your life miserable. In many instances, it was probably a sacrifice to agree to play for the show. If yours is an amateur production, simply be grateful that you have an orchestra at all.

Consult with the music director as soon as possible after every orchestra-only rehearsal. Review with him any aspect of the music that directly affects the production. Tell the music director immediately about any changes you make that might conceivably affect the music. Keep the lines of communication open. Otherwise, mind your own business and let the music director and the musicians do their work.

CAST AND ORCHESTRA REHEARSALS

If at all possible, schedule a "music only" rehearsal with the cast and orchestra before the first orchestra rehearsal. This lets the music director stop to help the singers find their notes in the orchestration and recognize their cues, balance the singers with the orchestra, set the correct tempos for the singers and dancers, and so on, without other distractions. This will also help the cast through the transition from piano-only accompaniment to full orchestra without the added stress of acting and dancing too. Schedule the music-only rehearsal a day or two in advance of the first orchestra rehearsal.

The first orchestra rehearsal with the entire company on stage should be a positive, energizing experience. Often, however, it turns out to be a bit of a let-down. Anticipation is so high that the stop-and-go nature of the rehearsal tends to dampen the cast's enthusiasm, drain their energy, and lessen the experience of singing and dancing to a live orchestra. Prepare the cast for this rehearsal with a little speech. Tell them what to expect, and ask them to be under-standing, cooperative, and *patient.* It's important to the show that all the music cues be exactly right, that tempos be worked out, that the balance of the orchestra and singers be properly adjusted, and so on.

The music director is essentially in charge of the first orchestra rehearsal. Let him accomplish what he needs to accomplish with the orchestra and the musical numbers. The dialogue sections of the show should run fairly smoothly. Even if they don't, forget about fix-ing anything during this rehearsal, including any technical problems. You will only make matters worse if you jump out of your seat every time something goes wrong. If anyone asks your opinion about something (they probably won't), by all means give it. Otherwise, sit back, relax, and let the rehearsal run its course.

It is essential that this rehearsal be devoted entirely to musical matters. The overriding consideration of the first orchestra rehearsal is the coordination of the orchestral music with the onstage activity—to establish tempos, cues, vocal/instrumental balance, length of in-cidental music for scene changes and transitions, and so on. All else that occurs in this rehearsal is secondary.

Expect a good deal of stopping and starting, mostly for benefit of the orchestra. Expect singers to forget their words, and to miss their cues. Expect the orchestra to be too loud. Expect the dancers to com-plain about the tempos as being either too fast or too slow. In short, expect that almost everything that *can* go wrong musically, *will* go wrong. You will be lucky, indeed, if you manage to get through the first act by the end of the scheduled rehearsal time.

Above all, remain calm. You knew that this was going to happen. This is not a big surprise. If you are mentally prepared for the evening, the potential damage to you and the production should be minimal.

When the scheduled time for the end of the rehearsal has come and gone, start to cut your losses. Send the orchestra home first, somewhere near the time when the rehearsal was *supposed* to have ended. If you planned ahead (as any good director should), you will have built an extra hour or so into the rehearsal.

Work with the cast with just the piano accompaniment for a lit-tle while after the orchestra has gone home, until you sense a point of diminishing returns. You'll know when you've reached that point. You've been there before during the regular rehearsal period. Send the cast home. They still have to remove their costumes and makeup, so they're looking at another half hour, at least, before they can get out of there.

Send the technicians and crew home last. They would stay there all night if you wanted them—you know they would—but even technicians have to sleep sometime. Kick everybody out, shut the place down, turn out the lights, and walk away.

It may be a little disconcerting for you to leave a rehearsal unfinished, with problems unresolved and questions unanswered, but it will not be fatal. As a matter of fact, a rehearsal like this can be beneficial for everybody. It usually brings a cast closer together. Their pride is at stake now, and they will do their absolute best to get through the next rehearsal, no matter what. They don't want to let you down. And if you managed to keep your wits about you, no one will have panicked.

Compared to the first orchestra rehearsal, the second orchestra rehearsal will seem like heaven, right? The orchestra will sound great. The singers will remember their lyrics. The dance tempos will be perfect. You'll just sit back and watch everything fall magically into place.

Wrong. You've been dreaming. Still, you should find the second orchestra rehearsal a vast improvement over the first one. It's the same production, of course, the same orchestra, the same cast and crew, the same director, but something altogether unexplainable and magical will have happened. Actually, it's not all that unexplainable. It's a matter of perspective, and of attitude.

Until now, the cast and crew have thought very little about performing for an audience. Their focus has been on learning lines and lyrics, remembering the blocking, painting the set, getting the light cues right, and getting the notes right. Suddenly, all that has changed.

At some point during the first orchestra rehearsal, it will have occurred to everyone connected with the production that this is serious. Soon, very soon, they are going to have to perform this show for *people*, real people sitting out there in those seats. In just a few days (perhaps even in a few hours, depending on how those last few rehearsals are going), this show is going up. All that has gone on before has simply been a prelude to the main event. For some actors, particularly the first-timers, this may come as a shock—a rather sudden and rude awakening. For other, more experienced members of the cast and crew, it will be a subtle shift in focus, a warm, familiar feeling that gradually overtakes them during the rehearsal.

TECHNICAL REHEARSALS

Just when you've gotten safely through the orchestra rehearsals, along comes another daunting proposition. Nevertheless, you can expect the technical rehearsals to proceed quite well. The technicians and stage crew have been working feverishly behind the scenes to prepare everything. A competent technical director will have arranged with the stage manager for "tech only" rehearsals, at which most of the technical bugs will have already been worked out. The light instruments are all hung and focused. Lighting cues have been run many times. (Some were probably run during your rehearsals, and you didn't notice.) Sound cues were run late at night, when nobody was around, so the sound crew could really crank up the volume. The stage crew has practiced moving the set, raising and lowering the drops, and setting the furniture and props. The stage manager has devised an efficient and foolproof cuing system for each of the technical elements of the show. It really is amazing what people can do if they're trusted to do their job and are left to their own devices to meet their own challenges.

As in a technical rehearsal for a straight play, do not interrupt the rehearsal except when there is imminent danger to life or limb. Stay in your seat, take notes, and simply marvel that it's going as well as it is. If you are on headset with the stage manager, designers, technical director, and/or technicians, restrain yourself. Speak only when spoken to, and let these people work it out themselves.

If you absolutely *must* stop the show, do so through the stage manager. The stage manager is in charge of running the show, not you, and what happens onstage and backstage is his responsibility now. Don't jump out of your seat and run down the aisle shouting *Stop! Stop!*, trailing your headset behind you (still plugged in, of course), notes flying everywhere, demanding that someone, *anyone, Fix it! Fix it!* The cast will be upset, their concentration broken; the stage manager will be quietly furious (notice that look you get as he walks slowly and deliberately from behind the curtain); and the orchestra will think you've gone mad. Control yourself. Your baby is growing up, and you've got to let it walk (and run) on its own.

Remind the music director/conductor not to interrupt the flow of the show except for *major* problems with the musical numbers and to press on, even if the singers forget their lyrics and the chorus is half a verse behind. The choreographer will be sitting next to you in the house, and since he is probably exhausted from rehearsals, will be content to sit quietly and take notes. It's the most rest he's had for weeks.

DRESS REHEARSALS

This is it—show time! You thought, perhaps, that opening night was show time, but you are mistaken. How the show looks in the dress rehearsals will be essentially what the audience sees opening night. Everything should be in good shape by now. (If you've come this far in this book, you *know* that everything will be under control, down to the smallest detail.) If it's not, if it's still "a little rough," you can make a few *minor* adjustments before opening, but for the most part, this show is as good as it's ever going to get.

Certainly the cast and crew will come alive with an audience out there, the intensity and excitement will jump up a level or two, and the rough edges will smooth themselves out a bit, but the basics—the staging, music, and choreography—are done, finished. If the production runs for longer than this weekend, you can make changes in rehearsal for *next* weekend, but for now, you've simply got to let . . . it . . . go. The cast, orchestra, technicians, and crew need to run this show at or as near as possible to performance conditions. The only difference between a performance and the dress rehearsal should be the presence of an audience. If there *is* an audience for the dress rehearsal—invited guests, for instance, or students—then the dress rehearsal is a performance and should be considered as such.

In any case, you've done your best. Take notes, or find some other way to amuse yourself. Sing along with the musical numbers, if you like. Dance in the aisles, if you must. Otherwise, sit back and enjoy the show.

In addition to the twelve-hour, put-it-all-together, technical-plus-orchestra-plus-makeup-and-costume-plus-dress-rehearsal marathon mentioned previously, some theatrical organizations are also quite fond of the "double dress"—two dress rehearsals on the same day, back-to-back, or with a short break in between. Certainly, as director, you've gotta do what you've gotta do to ensure that the show opens in reasonably good shape. But what about the shape of the actors and the crew? One dress rehearsal a day is taxing enough to mind and body, but two rehearsals in the same day, even with a reasonable break between them, can be devastating—particularly to singers' voices. (If they only sing half-voice to save their pipes, it's not really a dress rehearsal.) You want your cast and crew at their absolute best for opening night, not in a state of shock, physically and emotionally drained.

Plan ahead. If there's no other way, fine. It is, however, a high price for your cast and crew to pay for *your* lack of organization and planning.

Notes on Rehearsals

Since the music and scripts are rented, cast members will think they can't write anything in them. Some will believe they can remember their blocking without having to write it down. Some will rely on other members of the cast to remind them of movement and blocking. Since rehearsals for scenes sometimes occur days or even weeks apart, however, the cast will forget their blocking from one rehearsal to the next unless they write it down, and valuable rehearsal time will be wasted trying to reconstruct it. Insist that each cast member bring a pencil to rehearsal and that they use it to write blocking and other performance cues in the script or music. Then schedule an "erasing party" before you return the scripts and scores to the rental agency.

At times you will find yourself working with inexperienced performers who have never done a musical before or who may never have even been on stage before. These people have absolutely no idea of what is going on. They have no sense of the magnitude of the endeavor. They have no awareness or understanding of what is expected of them. They are blissfully unaware of the task that lies ahead, which may be just as well. They are naive, certainly, but eager, willing, and open to the experience.

It is your responsibility, as a representative of the noble theatrical art (and as a member of the human race), to help these extraordinary people learn what they need to know to function in this environment and to derive the greatest personal fulfillment in doing so. This does not mean you have to do all the training yourself. Approach some of the more experienced performers in your cast and ask them to serve as mentors, to help train and guide those who are newly arrived in the fascinating world of musical theatre. If your prospective mentors agree, pair them with a less experienced member of the cast. Check in with the pair occasionally to answer questions and to offer encouragement and support. You will find that this arrangement works remarkably well, both for you and for them. The performers often develop lasting friendships, and you don't have to use rehearsal time to explain procedures and expectations.

Enforce all memorization deadlines. Anything that gets away from the cast as they go along will be very hard to recover at some later date. Some first-time performers don't seem to realize that memorization requires a conscious effort. Perhaps they think the lines and the lyrics will somehow magically implant themselves in their memories while they sleep. They may be equally unaware that the seemingly effortless magic of the theatre is actually the result of incredibly hard work extending back over several weeks or months. It's a disconcerting realization for some, a disillusion in the truest sense of the word, but it's a lesson that must be learned.

Also enforce punctuality. Some performers may not realize the importance of always being on time, prepared, and ready to go; they think it's enough to show up at the scheduled time. Performers must not be allowed to come and go at will. Remind them to sign in on the callboard when they arrive at the theatre for rehearsal, and to check in with the stage manager whenever they leave the rehearsal hall for any reason. It's important that the stage manager knows where they are and that they can be reached on a moment's notice should their presence be required on stage.

It's the stage manager's responsibility to enforce discipline among the cast and crew, of course, but an occasional word from you will make his job much easier. Many problems that you and the stage manager will face are simply a matter of the performers' inexperience or lack of understanding of the production process. Some members of the cast may not understand the stage manager's role in the production, for example, and may resent being disciplined or corrected by anyone other than the director. You may need to set the record straight about that.

Give the members of your cast every opportunity to correct any of their negative behaviors. Have the stage manager speak with them individually, or speak with them yourself. Remember that this may be their first theatrical experience, *ever*. They may simply not know what's going on, or how to behave.

Discuss any discipline or attitude problems you encounter with the music director and choreographer. Enlist their aid in counseling the offender(s). In spite of your best efforts, however, it may become necessary to replace one or more members of the cast who are unable or unwilling to fulfill their responsibilities. They may be habitually late, unprepared for rehearsals, unresponsive or resistant to direction, disruptive, or simply incapable of functioning within the theatrical environment. For whatever reason, such behavior cannot be allowed to continue. In a large cast, self-discipline is of utmost importance. Those who lack it must necessarily be asked to leave. There is far too much to be done, in far too little time, with far too many people, to allow one person to disrupt the work of everyone else.

Do not proceed unilaterally in dismissing a cast member, of course; first consult the music director and choreographer. Expect the same consideration from them should they encounter their own problems with cast members.

SAMPLE REHEARSAL SCHEDULE

As with directing a play, the quality of your musical production is determined to a great extent by the quality of the rehearsal process. The quality of the rehearsal process is determined to a great extent by the organizational and management skills of the director. Since every musical has different requirements and every producing organization has different needs, there can be no definitive or "standard" rehearsal schedule for a musical. The sample musical rehearsal schedule in

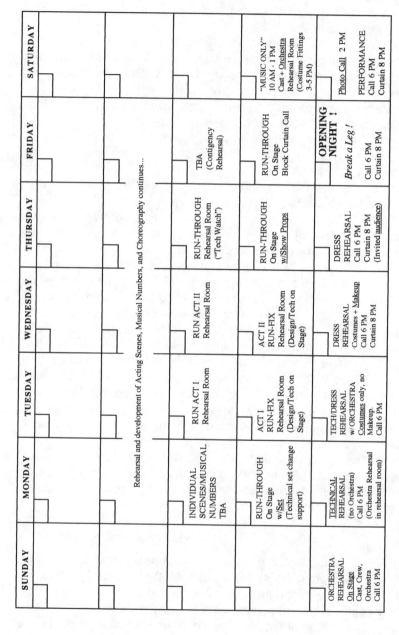

SUNDAY	MONDAY	TUESDAY	WEDNESDAY	THURSDAY	FRIDAY	SATURDAY
Rehearsal and development of Acting Scenes, Musical Numbers, and Choreography continues…						
	INDIVIDUAL SCENES/MUSICAL NUMBERS TBA	RUN ACT I Rehearsal Room	RUN ACT II Rehearsal Room	RUN-THROUGH Rehearsal Room ("Tech Watch")	TBA (Contigency Rehearsal)	"MUSIC ONLY" 10 AM - 1 PM Cast + Orchestra Rehearsal Room (Costume Fittings 3-5 PM)
	RUN-THROUGH On Stage w/Set (Technical set change support)	ACT I RUN-FIX Rehearsal Room (Design/Tech on Stage)	ACT II RUN-FIX Rehearsal Room (Design/Tech on Stage)	RUN-THROUGH On Stage w/Show Props	RUN-THROUGH On Stage Block Curtain Call	
ORCHESTRA REHEARSAL On Stage Cast, Crew, Orchestra Call 6 PM	TECHNICAL REHEARSAL (no Orchestra) Call 6 PM (Orchestra Rehearsal in rehearsal room)	TECH/DRESS REHEARSAL w/ ORCHESTRA Costumes only; no Makeup. Call 6 PM	DRESS REHEARSAL Costumes + Makeup Call 6 PM Curtain 8 PM	DRESS REHEARSAL Call 6 PM Curtain 8 PM (Invited audience)	OPENING NIGHT! Break a Leg! Call 6 PM Curtain 8 PM	Photo Call 2 PM PERFORMANCE Call 6 PM Curtain 8 PM

Figure 5–3. Musical Rehearsal Schedule

Figure 5–3 provides general guidelines for only the last few weeks of rehearsals. You will need to tailor the balance of the schedule to suit the musical you're doing and your own production situation.

How you get to these last few weeks in the rehearsal schedule is up to you. Work backward in preparing your schedule, as you would in scheduling rehearsals for a play. You will find that if you have scheduled the final weeks of rehearsal reasonably well, the preceding weeks will fall easily into place. Work within a consistent range of expectations for each element of the production—acting, music, and dance—to arrive at a workable and reasonable rehearsal schedule. Never be afraid of demanding or expecting too much of yourself, of your designers, technicians, and crew, and of your actors. Artistry and success don't come from expecting too little.

Note that in the last two weeks of rehearsals the sample schedule follows the one-new-thing-at-a-time format. (New things are underlined the first time they appear.) This may not always be possible, of course, but with a little planning you can probably manage to keep surprises to a minimum.

Consider increasing the number of contingency rehearsals in your rehearsal schedule. Anything can happen, and probably will. You must be prepared for unexpected and usually time-consuming problems. One contingency rehearsal every two weeks ought to do it. Schedule more if you feel particularly anxious or insecure.

Planning a rehearsal schedule for a musical is time-consuming. Your efforts will be well rewarded, however. Shortcuts in preparation and planning invariably result in time lost in rehearsal, and a lowering of the quality of the production.

Advice to the
Players

Very few college theatre majors aspire to be arts administrators or theatre managers. Students are more often interested in pursuing careers as actors, directors, designers, or choreographers, and they fail to realize the advantage to their careers that training in theatre management affords them.

There is a very limited market for directors who "just direct," and most of those positions are in the professional theatre. The majority of aspiring directors will work in other than professional organizations—with educational and community theatres and with other amateur organizations. This is not entirely a matter of quality, skills, or experience. It is simply a reflection of the marketplace—there are a very small number of positions available for directors in the professional theatre. As a director in an amateur theatre organization, you will assume, as a matter of course, many administrative and managerial responsibilities. It seems only reasonable to urge aspiring directors to acquire as much training and experience in theatre management as possible.

Many college and university theatre training programs offer courses in theatre management, and some require management courses as part of the curriculum for directors. This is to be applauded and encouraged. Even a single management course can prove invaluable to the first-time director, as well as to the experienced director who would like to expand his range of employable skills. If you are unable to enroll in theatre management courses, then read, study, and learn. There are a number of excellent books on theatre management listed in the bibliography. At the very least, teach yourself the basics of theatre management and essential management skills, so that when you're called upon to use them, you'll be prepared.

You might consider attaching yourself to a theatrical organization in order to learn management skills (or any other skills, for that matter) firsthand. Volunteer to assist the producer or general manager to learn the "biz" from the management point of view. Explore the available internships offered by many professional theatre companies and other arts organizations, and apply for any that will fulfill your training objectives.

Afterword

irecting a play or a musical is a marvelous and exciting journey. The journey starts with an idea, a vision—barely formed, but compelling. A decision is made to undertake the journey, and a personal commitment is made to see it through to the end. Traveling companions are chosen, a course is charted, and with no more supplies than can be carried inside one's head and heart, the adventure begins.

There are tentative first steps—testing the path (and one's skills), finding the way. Then, lengthening strides—strong, and self-assured. The incredible discoveries at every turn. The roads not taken (perhaps on the next journey) and the disappointments, great and small, each one a valuable lesson. Pressing on—renewed, confident, and undeterred—striving to meet demands and fulfill expectations. Those last, few difficult steps. And the grand moment of arrival, at last, that long-sought, long-awaited journey's end—opening night—the realization of only a few weeks of hard work or the culmination of a lifetime of dedicated effort.

Every member of the production team, cast, and crew makes a journey, too, each in his own way, each with her own personal goals, but with a common vision and a common, yet-unknown destination—a destination only the director can see. The director shares in all those separate journeys. In fact, without her fellow travelers, the director couldn't take even one step of her own. She is as dependent on them to make the journey as they are on her to point the way.

Oddly enough, it is the journey, not the destination, that is the source of greatest fulfillment. The goal, once reached, is quickly replaced by a higher goal—more distant, more elusive, more challenging. Every destination, every opening night, is the beginning of the next journey, another step along the path of an artist's life.

In any artistic endeavor, there are always the elements of chance and risk, the sense of uncertainty that the journey is worth taking, that the path is the right one, that the goal is worth reaching. For dedicated artists, the journey is its own reward; it is the artist's reason for being, and becoming, an artist.

Enjoy the journey.

Appendix A

"Who's in What"—Macbeth

CHARACTER	ACT ONE SCENE							ACT TWO SCENE				ACT THREE SCENE						ACT FOUR SCENE			ACT FIVE SCENE							
	1	2	3	4	5	6	7	1	2	3	4	1	2	3	4	5	6	1	2	3	1	2	3	4	5	6	7	8
First Witch	X		X													X		X										
Second Witch	X		X													X		X										
Third Witch	X		X													X		X										
Duncan		X		X		X																						
Malcolm		X		X		X				X										X				X		X	X	X
Donalbain		X		X		X				X																		
Lennox		X		X		X				X		X			X		X	X				X		X		X		X
Captain		X																										
Ross		X	X	X		X					X	X			X				X	X				X		X	X	X
Angus			X	X																		X		X		X	X	X
Macbeth			X	X	X		X	X	X	X		X	X		X			X					X		X		X	X
Banquo			X	X		X		X		X		X		X	X													
Lady Macbeth					X	X	X		X	X		X	X		X						X							
Fleance								X						X														
Porter										X																		
Macduff										X	X									X						X	X	X
Old Man											X																	
Murderer 1												X		X	X													
Murderer 2												X		X														
Murderer 3														X														
Servant/Male					X			X				X							X				X					
Servant/Female																					X							
Hecate																X		X										
Lord(s)		X										X			X		X					X		X				
Child/Apparition																		X										
Kings/Apparition																		X										
Lady Macduff																			X									
Macduff's Son																			X									

153

Appendix B

Casting Questionnaire

Name _____

Address _____

City _____ State _____ Zip _____

Phone (____) _____ Message (____) _____

Note: It is extremely important that you complete this questionnaire accurately. Please do not try to second-guess what the casting director may want from you in the way of appearance, skills, and so on. The questionnaire will work best for you if you provide correct information. It is clearly not in your best interest to be cast in a role or given an assignment based on false information.

Age: _____

Sex:

    __ Male

    __ Female

Build:

    __ Slender

    __ Medium

    __ Heavy

Height (to nearest inch): _____

Weight: _____

Hair Color (Natural):

    __ Bald/partial balding

    __ Moustache

    __ Beard

Eye Color (Natural): _____

    __ Colored Contacts

        Color: _____

Vocal Range:
__ Bass
__ Baritone
__ Tenor
__ Alto
__ Mezzo
__ Soprano

Fluent Dialects or Accents (check all applicable):
__ British
__ Cockney
__ Cuban
__ Deep South
__ French
__ German
__ Indian (India)
__ Irish
__ Italian
__ Jewish
__ Mexican
__ New England
__ New York
__ Puerto Rican
__ Russian
__ Scandinavian
__ Scottish
__ Spanish
__ Texan
__ West Indian

Vocal Style:
__ Broadway
__ Folk
__ Opera
__ Pop
__ Rock
__ Rap
__ Heavy Metal
__ Soul/Gospel

Dance Training/Ability (check all applicable):
__ Ballet
__ Ballroom
__ Belly
__ Break
__ Disco
__ Flamenco
__ Folk
__ Jazz
__ Mime
__ Swing/Jitterbug
__ Tap

Instruments you Play:

Interests (check all applicable):
__ Acting
__ Video Commercials
__ Film
__ Television
__ Radio Commercials/Voice-overs
__ Modeling
__ Beauty Contests
__ Bodybuilding

Experience or Training (check all applicable):
__ Acting
__ Video Commercials
__ Film
__ Television
__ Radio Commercials/Voice-overs
__ Modeling
__ Beauty Contests
__ Bodybuilding
__ Magician
__ Comedian/Stand-up
__ Musician

Experience:
List recent, significant, relevant experience only (last 6–12 months).

Date	Producer/Producing Organization	Role or Assignment
_____	_____	_____
_____	_____	_____
_____	_____	_____

Other Information/Skills/Interests:

Are you interested in backstage or behind-the-camera work (check all applicable):

☐ Lighting Technician   ☐ Lighting Crew
☐ Set Construction   ☐ Set Crew   ☐ Running Crew
☐ Costume Construction   ☐ Costume Crew/Dresser
☐ Makeup   ☐ Assistant Director   ☐ Stage Manager
☐ Floor Director   ☐ Radio/TV Technician   ☐ Cameraman
☐ Video Technician   ☐ Radio/TV crew

Male:
Suit Size ___ Shirt Size ___-___
Waist ___ Inseam ___
Shoe Size ___

Female:
Measurements ___ ___ ___
Dress/Suit Size ___ Skirt ___ Blouse ___
Slacks/Pants ___ Hose/Tights ___
Shoe Size ___

Please submit with this questionnaire:
- recent head shot (actors, singers, musicians).
- recent full body and head shot (dancers, models, bodybuilders).

You may also submit a recent, brief resume (one page only).

Bibliography

Allensworth, Carl. 1982. *The Complete Play Production Handbook.* Rev. ed. New York: Harper and Row.

Ball, William. 1984. *A Sense of Direction.* New York: Drama Book.

Bellman, Willard F. 1983. *Scene Design, Stage Lighting, Sound, Costume, and Makeup.* New York: Harper and Row.

Bowman, Walter Parker, and Robert Hamilton Ball. 1961. *Theatre Language.* New York: Theatre Arts.

Carter, Paul. 1988. *Backstage Handbook.* 2d ed. New York: Broadway.

Cavanaugh, Jim. 1973. *Organization and Management of the Nonprofessional Theatre.* New York: Richards Rosen.

Cohen, Edward M. 1988. *Working on a New Play.* Englewood Cliffs, NJ: Prentice Hall.

Cohen, Robert. 1981. *Acting Professionally.* 2d ed. New York: Barnes & Noble.

Dean, Alexander. 1926. *Little Theatre Organization and Management.* New York: Appleton-Century-Crofts.

Dean, Alexander, and Lawrence Carra. 1980. *Fundamentals of Play Directing.* 4th ed. New York: Holt, Rinehart and Winston.

Engel, Lehman. 1983. *Getting the Show On.* New York: Shirmer.

Farber, Donald C. 1981. *Producing Theatre: A Comprehensive Legal and Business Guide.* New York: Limelight Editions.

Greenberg, Jan Weingarten. 1981. *Theater Business.* New York: Holt, Rinehart and Winston.

Grote, David. 1986. *Staging the Musical.* Englewood Cliffs, NJ: Prentice Hall.

Gruver, Bert. 1972. *The Stage Manager's Handbook.* Rev. ed. New York: Drama Book.

Hays, David. 1989. *Light on the Subject.* New York: Limelight Editions.

Hodge, Francis. 1982. *Play Directing.* 2d ed. Englewood Cliffs, NJ: Prentice Hall.

Hoggett, Chris. 1975. *Stage Crafts.* New York: St. Martin's.

Katz, Judith A. 1981. *The Business of Show Business.* New York: Barnes & Noble.

Langley, Stephen. 1974. *Theatre Management in America.* New York: Drama Book.

Learcroft, Richard, and Helen Learcroft. 1984. *Theatre and Playhouse.* London: Methuen.

Nelms, Henning. 1958. *Play Production.* New York: Barnes & Noble.

Newman, Danny. 1977. *Subscribe Now!* New York: Theatre Communications Group.

Plummer, Gail. 1961. *The Business of Show Business.* New York: Harper.

Smith, Milton. 1948. *Play Production.* New York: Appleton-Century-Crofts.

Stern, Lawrence. 1979. *School and Community Theatre Management.* Boston: Allyn and Bacon.

———. 1982. *Stage Management.* Boston: Allyn and Bacon.

Telford, Robert S. 1983. *Handbook for Theatrical Production Managers.* New York: Samuel French.

Tumbusch, Tom. 1969. *Complete Production Guide to Modern Musical Theatre.* New York: Richard Rosen.